LEARNING TO RIDE AGAIN

LEARN-ING TO RIDE AGAIN

Amanda Stephens

Fedd Books
P.O. Box 341973
Austin, TX 78734
www.thefeddagency.com

Published in association with The Fedd Agency, Inc., a literary agency.

ISBN: 978-1-943217-38-0
eISBN: 978-1-943217-39-7

Printed in the United States of America
First Edition 15 14 13 10 09 / 10 9 8 7 6 5 4 3 2

To my family who ran alongside me
until I could pedal on my own.

PROLOGUE

It was New Year's Eve 2011, nine months after Dustin's death, and Doug, our department's customer experience guru, dropped a piece of paper on my desk. It was a recipe for Hopping John. With a little ham, dry onion soup mix, water, Tabasco, and of course black-eyed peas, you could whip up a year of good fortune! Ironically, I'd lived most of my adult life without even knowing that black-eyed peas were a staple of New Year's Eve dining along with a few other luck-bringing dishes. Hopping John. I glanced over the recipe, and for a brief second a wave of panic hit me. We hadn't eaten any black-eyed peas the year before! The silly revelation somehow struck a painful cord. I've never been superstitious, and even now, I know it's all nonsense. But sometimes the subconscious search for, "Why?" takes you to irrational places.

On our first New Year's together as a married couple, a co-worker finally schooled me on the New Year's significance of black-eyed peas. At ten till 5:00 p.m., she was looking up recipes online and shouting them down the hallway so we all could benefit from her research and eventually bask in the luck the new year would bring. That night, on my way home, I bought my first can of black-eyed peas.

The peas never quite made it to the table. They were upstaged by a tantalizing spread of corn dogs, clam chowder, cheddar biscuits, and sparkling cider.

For Dustin, the kitchen was his laboratory. Now I loved to cook as well, but Dustin loved to *create*. He was always tackling new techniques for old classics and coming up with a few originals of his own. Earlier we'd decided to have a lazy New Year's Eve, but, oh, what to make for dinner? Our Friday norm had become dinner and a movie, and this night was no different. I'd call him from my office and say, "So what do you want for dinner?" which would begin a lengthy discussion weighing our various options. On this night, Dustin decided he wanted to tackle corn dogs; he'd never made them from scratch before. While the familiar fair food was one of his favorites, it was one of my least, which only further fueled the fire. He would make a corn dog to shame all other corn dogs and convert his very skeptical wife. How can you argue with such passion and resolve? New Year's Eve or not, we were having corn dogs, and I couldn't help but smile.

My contribution to the menu was less about taste and more about utility—utility of Christmas presents that is. My mom had given me a set of special ceramic soup bowls that were designed with a separate compartment for crackers or bread, and I wanted to play with my toy. For dessert we would have red velvet cake baked in white heat-resistant coffee cups, another Christmas gift. I was giddy anticipating the darling presentation of our dishes while Dustin was busy perfecting his batter. It was one of the few nights we both worked in the kitchen together, and as with almost every meal, we staged the big reveal. Dustin took pictures from every angle—not uncommon when he was particularly proud of his presentation—and then we settled in on the couch for a lovely, lazy evening.

Although I do still have the pictures of our tray of goodies, my favorite memento from that night is our "family picture," the only one we took. Shortly after we'd sat down, the cats joined us on the couch, cuddling side-by-side as they did. Dustin somehow was able to get a picture of all of us on the couch together, quite a feat for a pre-selfie stick era. I love that picture; it captured the essence of many of our nights. Yes, those cozy, uneventful nights watching movies with "the babies"—I wouldn't trade them for anything. I made sure the family portrait made it into the video at the memorial.

I would not be making Hopping John for New Year's. In fact, I rather defiantly determined I would not purchase any of the dreaded beans. Never mind that I usually didn't give them a second thought on any occasion—that evening I chose to spit in the face of canned luck.

I'd become rather disenchanted with the whole New Year's hoopla. Really, it's the difference of one day. We go from p.m. to a.m., a Saturday becomes a Sunday, and yet supposedly there's some cosmic shift that magically changes the course of your life in a split second? Right. It's just like when it's your birthday, and someone asks you if you feel any older. Really? Why do we ask inane questions like that? We're all so desperate for a fresh start that we embrace the season as a cleansing from the gluttony of the previous month or months, but as sure as it could be the year where everything clicks, it could also be the year life falls apart.

More so than Christmas, the week leading up to that New Year's had been particularly difficult. All the trite expressions casually thrown around hit my ears like lead balloons. About 2011, "Boy, this year just flew by, didn't it?" No, not at all. "Gosh, you blink, and then the year's gone." Tried blinking it away many times, but to my dismay, it didn't go away.

Yet even those who acknowledged that the year was long and difficult couldn't help but drink the New Year's Kool-Aid. "I am ready for 2012; 2011 just needs to be over." Though I somewhat agreed with the later statement, the former brought no comfort either. Though I faced the end of a calendar year, March 21, 2012 would mark the end of another year, a year of dreadful firsts.

New Year's Eve started the countdown for an anniversary I wasn't sure I was ready to face. It would be a year Dustin would not be in. As much as 2011 hurt, I had memories of Dustin there, starting with our January 1st lunch at Katz's Deli in Austin, the day before it shut its doors after 30 years. We'd gone there on our honeymoon, and he wanted one last pastrami sandwich. I wanted to savor the memory of our midnight meal the year before. That was a good day, and there were others.

For a time in 2011, I was married. For all of 2012, I would be a widow. I had this precious two-year capsule of memories that each passing year would threaten to fade, and it frightened me that I might forget pieces of our life. So on a night when most were celebrating with family and friends, I chose to stay in with my laptop. I couldn't stop the year from coming or the subsequent years after, but I could type away some of my fears by telling our story, just as God was beginning to write the next chapter of mine. With every key stroke, I released hidden memories, giving them voice and permanence on the page.

Grief

1

In a noisy, small town junior high gymnasium, my father-in-law leaned over to me in the bleachers during my niece's volleyball game and said, "I always regretted calling you that night and telling you about Dustin over the phone. If I'd have only waited a little bit longer, someone would've been there with you. You didn't need to hear it over the phone . . . by yourself. I regretted it the minute I hung up."

I knew I responded to him because I felt my lips move and smiled understandingly. After all, it had been nearly three years at that point, but my heart began to thump a familiar pounding. I was remembering. The wound that years had begun to heal, the scene that was filed away, and the emotions talked through, written out and saved for memories, flooded the brain. I sat on the cold, hard bleacher, cognizant of the game being played before me, but my mind had left the building, dragging my heart to the night when life changed.

That night. That phone call. Yes, of course . . . that conversation, that dagger. The quiet . . . because, no, no one was there but me, me waiting for Dustin to return my call. (He was three hours north in Tyler visiting a friend.) That moment trying to process and be calm while staring at my reflection in the guest room mirror as a stranger stared back. Phone to ear . . . eyes wide, skin pale . . . no longer a wife. The heart pounding, the thumping echoing in my ears making it difficult to hear the answers to questions impossible to ask. The shaky dial to my parents and the choking on my words like a foreign language, like a mute trying to form audible sound—the words you shouldn't have to say. "Mom, Dustin is dead." The screams because my mom did not understand this language either and upon questioning, the shrill snap, "He's *dead*!"

The room was eerily still. I summoned the wailing I felt in the deepest pit of my soul, but no sound came forth, so I paced. I went first to the bedroom, pulled out my overnight bag and began to fill it with unrelated items as my mind raced. *I've got to get to Tyler. Yes, I need to be there; that's what you should do of course.* Wandering aimlessly around the room. Stop. Stooping over onto the bed gripping the comforter. *I can't do this, God. I . . . I can't.* Deep breath. Regroup. Continuing to pack, pausing to stare at the bag trying to make sense of its contents. *This is what I'll be expected to do. Someone will take me there or tell me what to do.* Sitting on the couch waiting, rocking, and waiting.

I knew it would be a while before my in-laws arrived, but my sister-in-law texted to say they were on the way. I called our pastor's wife, one of my dearest friends, also slightly related to the Stephens clan. Ringing. She answered.

"I . . ." pausing for air and words.

"I know, baby, we're coming right now," she said.

"Ohhh ok. Good." I felt like a five-year-old left home alone.

Not long after that, the apartment began to swell with people, mostly family, but bodies nonetheless and too many of them. We hugged; we cried. I think I cried. I must have cried. I desperately tried to cry because, of course, I was expected to cry. I remember watching my mother-in-law doubled over in agony, and I felt like I watched from the window though I stood right beside her, like I was watching the scene play out but was confused by my part. I strangely recall trying to make small talk with my brother-in-law. He's not one for emotion or expression, and I talk when uncomfortable or nervous. Of course he felt deeply in that moment, but I think when tragedy strikes the unprepared, we default to personality autopilot.

There had never been so many people in our apartment at one time, and to accommodate the crowd, some migrated into the guest bedroom. *Was it clean? Where were the cats?* I walked around casually picking up minor odds and ends as if it made a difference. *Are there bills lying out by the computer? Should I put them away?* Of all emotions to entertain, I felt embarrassed that our home wasn't more in order, but then again, I hadn't expected any guests that night.

Regardless of the delivery, my father-in-law's news would've still shattered my heart, as I know it did his. Furthermore, I presume that not even the company of dear friends could have tempered the blow or lessened the pain. Friends, although a comfort, can do little for the shock when it hits, but they are a lifeline for every step thereafter.

My parents wouldn't arrive till after I was asleep due to the seven-hour commute. Was I really asleep? I don't know. Exhaustion likely carried me in and out of the cruel consciousness that was now life. I heard muffled voices in the living room, and then light filtered into my bedroom as the door opened. Mom was there. Papa was right beside her of course, but as a child instinctively runs to mom with their scrapes and cuts, so my heart freely bled at the embrace of her arms and coo of her voice. I didn't get up. I just lay there and cried. We all laid there and cried. I didn't need to be strong then, and I didn't try.

The next morning I felt hungover—heavy with sadness as the shock began to settle into grief. I opened the bedroom door slowly. The living room was bright and airy, not dark and smothering as the night before, tempting me to imagine a different fate awaited me. My dad was headed out to run an errand while my friend was making phone calls in the corner. It felt like one of my many sleepwalking episodes where in a half-dream state, I intrude upon activity bustling around me, hoping no one notices that I'm strangely still in my pajamas. But I was awake.

In the breakfast nook, a beautiful arrangement of flowers seemed to stretch the radius of the table, a gift from my beloved cousin in California. I marveled at their presence. It had only been hours it seemed since the news, yet he'd moved heaven and earth to make sure I woke to beauty that day. I collapsed into a chair, tired already, but content to be near them. It was the first of many times to come that unexpected expressions of love would alter the course of my day and provide glimmers of hope. My mom sat still on the couch, reading. She was always reading, books of every genre but mostly the Bible.

"His Word, Amanda; I love His Word," she said. She said it with such reverence that I listened and leaned in. "Will you let me read this to you?" she asked.

I did that morning, and the next, and the next. And each morning, it seemed a new revelation awaited in the pages, new mercies to be sure. I let her spoon feed me truth. If I was ever to get through that week, I would need nourishment, but I lacked the heart and motivation to reach for my own Bible, so we heard from hers. Despite the fog, there was clarity in the scriptures I had not known before, and I hungered for more to answer my questions and give purpose to my pain.

Sitting at the funeral home, I heard the funeral director's voice and felt his compassionate eyes looking at me, but how strange that I, a woman still in her twenties, would be making these decisions. I listened and tried to absorb the options and costs while staring blankly at a catalogue of caskets. Wasn't it just a little more than a year ago we were flipping through albums with pictures of wedding cakes of all shapes, flavors, and colors making the decisions engaged couples make? How did we go from chocolate or vanilla to bronze or solid maple? I nodded along as best as I could, until I couldn't, and I turned my head toward the window at my left and whimpered helplessly into my shoulder. My friend, who'd sat quietly in the back of the room, immediately rallied to my side and towered over me as a protection. She's six feet tall, so she towers over most people, let alone five-foot-three me, but her protective stance gave me just enough cover and courage to compose myself and do what needed to be done.

Once our options were established and I had notes to take back to the rest of the family, there was the business of bringing Dustin home. Home for Dustin now took on a whole new meaning; I gathered that. He really was already home, but there was the need in our hearts for us to grieve him here. Yes, it was just a body, merely a shell, but I knew I had to see him, had to hold him at the risk of what that final impression might leave. It was, for me, the most painful dagger of the whole thing. He died miles from me of relatively unknown causes, in the house of a man I barely knew, and waited for me cold, surrounded by strangers. They said he would arrive Thursday and be ready for viewing on Friday. I would see him by myself, no distractions, no forced pretense, just good-byes.

• • •

In a dismal funeral parlor room time stood still, and my heart crossed realms. I can't tell you what happened in that room that day, not all of it at least. Some things are sacred and reserved for the heart. At the same time, there was a magnificence I've longed to capture in words, but the adjectives evade me even now, years later. It was like going into the Holy Place, so often described of the Jewish temple in the Old Testament, a place and ground so holy even the high priests feared to tread and did so solemnly. Yet each year, they stepped through the veil to meet with God, the only place His presence was found.

On this day there were no veils or curtains, just a door. There was no grand altar or candles or incense, just a small room, a chair, and a sleeping man, my man. My parents and brother walked in with me, and we stood together. They were there at first to support me, standby in case I had a complete meltdown, but I was calm, and though grateful for their support, was ready to be left alone.

That morning I awoke sensing purpose in the day. I was very intentional in dressing as if this was the date of our lives, and *everything* had to be perfect. I wanted to be cute, yet comfortable. My hair was freshly colored and straight like he liked it. I wore jeans for comfort and for sentimentality, I chose the floral top I wore the night I told Dustin I loved him. I've never worn it since. Upon first glance, I was very grateful they didn't have Dustin in a coffin but rather a tall cot of sorts covered in a heavy green blanket. I remember thinking I was glad he had that big, green blanket because it was cold inside.

He was sleeping. To the outside world, I was going to say goodbye to the body of my husband, but I came to that room to watch him sleep. As soon as my family left the room, I pulled over the big arm chair from the corner so I could be right by his side. I thought I'd have so many things to say in my short hour, but in that moment little came to mind. It was a moment of pure contentment. I stared at him with awe. He wasn't stilted or positioned; he was relaxed, at rest. I had not received a vision of Dustin smiling and dancing in heaven as some do of a loved one passed, but I was watching a physical representation of the peace and rest I knew he now felt in his spirit. It was the most calming, almost tangible, stillness I've ever felt. For a while, I dared not move. I felt as much as love was gently flowing from my heart to his, love was pouring back into my soul.

I felt like Dustin was there—and not just the "sleeping" Dustin. Maybe I've watched too many episodes of *Touched by an Angel* in my day, and I could never pinpoint a spot, but in a place that should've been like a tomb to me, I felt more alive than I'd ever felt before or since. These are the experiences where facts do little to support the story changed lives tell.

I'd brought my Bible with me just in case. Seemed like the right thing to do at the time, given the circumstances. I thought I would need to console myself through the Word, but in those moments, I didn't need consoling. We were having a sweet time, all things considered, so as he'd said to me so many nights before when we'd read the Bible before bed, I said, "Well, what shall we read? Romans? Romans is always good." With no agenda in mind, I flipped carelessly over to Romans. I landed on chapter four, the faith chapter I'd read countless times in the months prior. The verse highlighted on the page said, "He is our father in the sight of God in whom he believed—the God who gives life to the dead and calls those things that are not as though they were." For a randomly-picked scripture, that verse and the verses to follow couldn't have been more perfect.

When the time came, I was able to leave with no qualms or hesitation. I kissed Dustin goodnight, not goodbye. I walked quietly out, waved farewell, and gently shut the doors; after all, he was sleeping. My mom said when I emerged from the room I was glowing. What I felt in my spirit, her statement confirmed. I'd been standing on holy ground. Looking back, the week Dustin died was the most devastating and glorious week of my life. I don't know how else to describe it. The shock and pain of losing him so unexpectedly was surreal and mind-numbing, only to be matched in intensity by the dichotomous day-to-day nearness of heaven. I wouldn't say I met Jesus for the first time that week, but we were certainly reintroduced, as though when Dustin entered eternity I was granted a glimpse of glory, and it followed me in the days to come.

2

The first year of marriage is affectionately coined the "Honeymoon Phase" for obvious reasons and illustrated by syrupy demonstrations of love. At the same, I've also heard, "The first year is the hardest," again for obvious reasons; a little combustion is bound to happen when two independent worlds become one. I tend to think the first year falls somewhere in between, but then I only have one year on which to base my assertions. Regardless of which side of the road your first year falls, there are endless conversations about the future, ranging from two kids or four to which toilet paper will ultimately grace the bathroom and your tooshies. Do we want to rent or buy, carpet or hardwood, office or nursery, and can we hire a maid to clean it all up? Must you eat cereal in bed? Cats or dogs . . . or both?! Thanksgiving with your parents, and Christmas with mine? Presents for all or presents for none? Are you listening? Are you ready? Will you still love me when we're old and gray? Because we *will* grow old and gray together . . .

And because you will grow old and gray together, you indulge only fun, optimistic conversations of the future and the occasional silly battles of the sexes. You make plans, endless plans, and dream, crazy dreams. You don't talk about wills. You don't talk about life insurance. You certainly don't discuss funerals and last wishes. Death doesn't even cross your mind because the Honeymoon Phase might as well be a force field shielding you of all trauma, difficult decisions and well, life. Even if you subscribe to the "hardest year" theory, your first-year self assumes this too shall pass, and one day, a wiser Mr. and Mrs. will testify to the old adages of a for-better-or-worse kind of love. You will grow old together after all, and these "adult" topics are for later—later when there are kids, property, and reality checks.

My new reality was the sudden invasion of family and friends into our space with hugs, tears, and searching eyes that I intentionally avoided. They silently searched for answers when I only had questions. It would be some time before I could verbalize my feelings because at that time I felt none. Shock insulated the hurt, and I feared waking from the coma with pain receptors engaged. After the chaos following the call, the apartment that once swelled with people and hysteria settled into a deceptive stillness. The calm and quiet were welcomed; the knowledge of what now remained was an unwelcomed guest. I sat on the couch next to my friend, Jaci, and she waited. I don't think either of us knew what to do next. We had not had this conversation either.

"Um, I think I'm a little hungry," I said.

"Ok, what are you hungry for? Anything . . . I'll get you anything," Jaci said.

I settled on Chick-fil-A. We sent my brother who had retreated to the guest room while we talked to run the errand. He'd spoken little that night, but, oh, a storm of silent emotions brewed inside. He was grateful for the reprieve. My parents would arrive later that evening, and I was vaguely aware that we would be going to the funeral home the next day to discuss options. There it was—the options no one had discussed, the options that were foreign to my brain, even then. I would be asked questions for which I had no answers, and worst of all, I would have to make decisions. I have always been relatively indecisive—not about really important things like God and personal convictions, but everything else. Please don't ask me to choose which restaurant to eat at or movie to watch. I'll debate with myself endlessly and torture myself in the event of the wrong decision. Dustin, on the other hand, was very decisive. He was quick to determine what he wanted and acted accordingly. Just two years prior, it was this same decisive young man who walked into a Belton, Texas, church and saw for the first time the woman he knew he was going to marry singing onstage, unaware of his presence or the impending pursuit. Pursue he did, undaunted by the slow mover who tried to keep his advances at arm's length, despite the pounding in her chest and blush on her cheeks. He'd made the decision to pursue her all the way to the altar where he promised in front of family and friends to love her for better or worse, in sickness and in health, and till death . . .

Parting like this was cruel, unexpected, and void of direction. I helplessly sorted through files of memories in my brain, catalogues of conversations, desperately hoping for an excerpt of some long-forgotten chat about our wishes should one of us pass before the other. It was not there. In life, I'd become dependent on him to navigate me through the decision-making process on many issues, be they deep or trivial. I marvel today at how patient he was to humor my lists of pros and cons and shoulder my laments of confusion and worry at the prospect of making the wrong decision.

Yes, patience was granted for decisions of the heart and mind, but the same did not hold true for decisions regarding the dinner table. It was not an unfamiliar scene at a restaurant to see me deliberate between multiple options as if I was negotiating a peace treaty and finally decide on something new and moderately adventurous. I would triumphantly tilt my chin a bit as I stated my order, knowing Dustin was shaking his head with a sly grin, anticipating this would not end well . . . for me. There was no swapping of plates when the inevitable order envy occurred. He promptly devoured his tried-and-true while I poked a fork at my adventurous.

"I knew you weren't going to like that," he'd say without pity. Depending on the day, I would either pretend to enjoy my meal out of spite or sulk while sneaking my fork onto his plate.

What would he say in this moment on the couch? What I

would give to sit across the table from him now. I felt ashamed that the person who was supposed to know him better than anyone else was at a complete loss.

Over nuggets and waffle fries, two friends sat and stared and occasionally talked. There was freedom on that couch to not have any answers, voice the bewilderment, talk through the practical, and dabble in the what-ifs. I know some report a dulling of the senses after such a shock, but I strangely recall the delicious taste of the bite-sized chicken and salty fries. I couldn't feed my hunger for answers, so I fed my rumbling tummy instead. I'd made at least one decision that night, and the control tasted good. I pretended this was just another girls' night that my brother randomly decided to crash, and as most girls' nights go, we were huddled on the couch with greasy goodness, Dr. Pepper, and conversation. Conversation. Decisions. Dustin. We spoke of him like he was just away for a bit. I think we even laughed at some point, because it's hard not to tell Dustin stories without laughter.

It was in the midst of laughter and the sweet pause to follow that I began to think with great clarity. No, we had not discussed burial preferences, but emptiness gnawed at my stomach when I thought of following a casket to a stone grave. It was not the emptiness of grief, but rather of the formality of the scene that seemed so foreign to the life of the man I knew—a man not of convention or elaborate tributes but of living outside of the box. I could not picture myself visiting a grave and talking to a marble nameplate, with hopes of connecting to this adventurous spirit who in his prime leaped with life.

I'd never been a proponent of cremation before, yet something stirred inside me when I thought of sharing what remained of Dustin with the world—a symbolic act of what I hoped to do with my memories and our story in the future. It would have to be an incredibly special place, of course, one uniquely worthy of him.

And then I knew. The plan came to me like a beautifully wrapped gift from heaven deposited into my heart. I declared with unusual certainty that I was going to take Dustin to California.

As much as I am a Texas girl, Dustin was a California dude. The Golden State was his first love after Jesus, and you could tell that within a short time of meeting him. Never mind his dusty blonde hair, surfer build, and blue eyes like the sea, he had the carefree, nomadic spirit of the West Coast. Though his family moved many times throughout his childhood, he spent most of the years in California, specifically Chico and Paradise. He would describe the Chico Farmer's Market to me in such a way that I could almost smell the aroma of flowers and herbs mixed with baked goods and other nefarious scents characteristic of the college scene. He would take me there, he said, and I so desperately wanted to go.

Just up the road was Paradise, a much smaller town surrounded by forest and mountainous terrain, and hidden somewhere in those mountains was a secret oasis anchored by a green, glassy pond. He spoke of this place with reverence, its beauty hidden and well-protected. He told me stories of jumping from the rocks into its deep, chilly waters. He'd hiked to this spot many times and longed to show it to me.

I really knew so little about this place, only a few random clues, but that night I knew with great certainty that it was to be his resting place. Though the map remained vaulted in his memory, I would find this place, and I would travel there, hike the trail, and take him home. I pictured his face forming a smirk of surprise at my plans. Though this was Dustin to a "t," this was not like me. But oh, what a labor of love. His slightly less audacious wife would defy tradition and embark on this quest in his honor. Yes, he would think this was very cool.

"Will you go with me, Seth? Will you make the hike with me?" I said. After thinking aloud to my friend, I suddenly shouted out with great conviction to my brother in the next room, certain he'd already picked up on my musings. The intimate nature of the journey longed for solitude, but the physical requirements demanded wisdom and a guide. My brother was an avid outdoorsman with a number of challenging hikes under his belt.

"Yes!" he said emphatically without hesitation, giving away the knot in his throat. This was something he could do. In the midst of helplessness, he'd been given a charge that matched his skills and gifted a much-needed outlet for brotherly love.

"I'll go with you, Manda," he reiterated with the conviction of the Tolkien fellowship, a Samwise Gamgee companion who would follow me to the depths of Mordor should it become necessary.

I smiled with genuine happiness. I would still respectfully gather options from the funeral home to present to his family, but I prayed . . . oh I prayed that they would embrace this journey and release me to go, entrusting me with their son and brother. Upon my decision, I felt an assurance in my soul of something at work. I knew so little in those early days, but as much as this journey would lead to his burial, I sensed it would also be the start of healing and life for me.

3

Though I have never birthed a child of my own, much to my dear mother's chagrin, *every last one* of my girlfriends has—well, just about. One of my best friends alone has four girls. Rabbits have nothing on her. She thinks "baby." *Bam!* She's pregnant. I've been very fortunate in life to have retained many of my close friendships throughout the years despite the separation of miles and really just life. As a result, I've had the privilege of walking through many of their pregnancies with them. Most women have their own unique pregnancy and birthing experiences. Just take a seat at any baby shower, and you'll hear mothers regale with stories of morning sickness, water breaking at the in-law's house, and the twenty-four hours of labor it took to bring junior into the world—battle scars at their best. However, the one thing I would venture to say all moms-to-be have in common is pregnancy exhaustion.

If you're a mom, you know exactly what I'm talking about.

There seems to be no rhyme or reason to it when it hits, and then some days, some weeks, it is constant. Ironically, you see it most in the first trimester long before the waddle weight and visible baby kicks.

Grief in some ways is like pregnancy, but without the payoff. Those first few weeks, months really, the exhaustion was beyond anything I'd ever experienced. I willed myself each day to get through the hours at work so I could collapse at home. It was the kind of tired where you find yourself talking to your legs, coaxing them to lift for the next step. Your eyelids may as well be sandbags, and your skin feels taut from the lack of sleep and subsequent excess of caffeine. At any time, I thought my body would spontaneously give way, and I would implode into a pile on the floor. The only thing I knew to compare it to, from what I'd viewed, was pregnancy exhaustion, and even that may be a pale comparison.

It first hit the afternoon of the memorial service, which was five days after Dustin had passed. The adrenaline leading up to the service thankfully fueled me through the many appointments, decisions, and visitations. It's a strange high that possesses you in those days, at least it was for me. I credit it to God's presence carrying me through the fire of those first few days and the wonder of heaven that somehow felt so real in those moments knowing Dustin had just crossed the threshold. It was a tangible sense of glory, and you strangely couldn't help but savor it despite the reason for its coming. But what goes up must come down.

I finished eating with extended family and guests in the fellowship hall at our church, and I could feel the waves coming and coming quickly. I needed quiet. Our pastor's wife helped me escape into the empty sanctuary. I vaguely recalled the dozens of flower arrangements lining the stage during the service and wanted to take a moment to appreciate the kindness of friends and strangers. She guided me along, and I became thankful for her arms around my waist because the adrenaline had officially run out. It was finished. Dustin was beautifully honored in the best way we could orchestrate, one piece of the process complete. Within an hour, I buried myself beneath the covers of my bed and slept . . . for a long time.

Though the afternoon nap was helpful, I was running on a weeklong deficit that felt more like a lifetime. I would run on fumes for many months to come. Living life—getting up and getting out—expended more energy than I thought possible, and I realized exhaustion was my new companion. I was a constant live wire in those days. By the end of the day, I'd have exhausted all my powers of restraint, so my poor mom often bore the brunt of my eruptions over the phone. One innocently misspoken word would trip the wire and BOOM—leaving her gun-shy and me feeling guilty and more drained from the impromptu outburst. I didn't even know where it came from half the time, but like a geyser, out would come these almost uncontrollable rants.

I've always been one who needed her sleep. I can be quite crabby without it, so it's not surprising that my lack of quality

REM led to my raw behavior. Nothing, I mean nothing, is more exhausting than the depth of emotions felt during loss. It's as if every tear saps strength as it slips down your face, draining any reservoir you might have had. It's why some people just choose not to feel because they know they can't function under the physical and emotional demands of indulging their pain.

To some degree, this was how I coped at work. I remember being surprisingly focused and productive my first week back in the office, only days after saying goodbye to my husband. Spring is my busiest season professionally, and being out for a week set me back. *Really?* I'm aware that my reflections sound cold, implying morbidly skewed priorities, but projects and busyness were my escape. I worked tirelessly to not fall behind and exhausted myself in the process. Come the weekend, I had no energy and fell victim to the grief demanding to be felt. Weekends, at times, were dark. I would retreat to my safe places with my safe people, and then, and only then, would I unload.

And after unloading, I would hurriedly pack it all back up, embarrassed by the spectacle of my sorrow, regretting the inconvenience of my ramblings and tired, very tired. No, sometimes it is truly easier not to feel, so instead, I made friends with the dark circles under my eyes that refused to fade. I would be present in body but often absent in mind and certainly spirit. Mondays dawned like Groundhog Day offering no rest for the weary.

The other side effect I've often heard my mom-to-be friends lament is what they call "pregnancy brain." I guess utter exhaustion and loss of mental acuity is a packaged deal. They might define pregnancy brain as the inability to concentrate, periodic lapses in memory, and the occasional incoherent thought. I understood that as well.

I felt like a child, like I was learning life again. I found simple tasks took twice as much time because I had to think through them; they no longer came naturally. *Did those tears wash away brain cells with them too?!* I desperately wanted to be and do as I did before, so I pushed myself very hard to cover up my failings. Once a natural conversationalist, I found myself weary of small talk. The time it took for my thoughts to connect and register, let alone be spoken, was agonizing. I felt like I was drowning in jello.

When you're pregnant, you get to laugh it off, and everyone laughs with you anticipating the joy to come. Playing the pregnancy card is somewhat reassuring because it assumes that in nine months the confusion will lesson, and at least some, if not all, of the highly functioning individual you knew yourself to be would return. The painful crescendo of contractions is released in a glorious moment of baby cries and adult tears. Many a friend has told me there is an immediate sense of physical relief once the baby is born, and for a moment, the agony of child birth is forgotten.

In grief, it's different. Sure you can play your own hand of cards, but the time frame is less certain. You are undoubtedly carrying a weight, but there is nothing to birth, no one act that releases you from the grade school intelligence and haze-like existence that now defines you. And the thought that this is your new normal terrifies you.

I recall listening to a song around this time with a line that alluded to babies and hearses and the sad juxtaposition of life events experienced by different people. It was a strangely comforting acknowledgement, though my reality lay with the hearses. I used what little energy I had to keep my dismal musings contained and bootstrapped my way to baby showers and weddings, celebrating new life cautiously.

I could tell there was a hesitancy that precipitated certain topics in my presence, one of them being babies. For some, I think the uncertain awkwardness surrounding such topics prompted unnecessary filler in a desperate attempt to reassure me and themselves that the dream of motherhood was not yet lost. They failed to realize I didn't want just any baby; I wanted Dustin's and my baby. I wanted to hold Bella or Jack in my arms while I shielded them from the endless flashes of the camera as their daddy chronicled every minute of newborn life. I wanted to see a little pink fishing pole propped against the tackle box in the garage and little aprons for our little messes in the kitchen. Though Dustin didn't like me being in the kitchen while he was cooking, I have a feeling he'd have made an exception for our little chef. I wanted to stare at that precious little face for hours and pick out the mommy and daddy features. I wanted . . . I want . . . what I can no longer have.

4

Those first couple of weeks, I felt like I heard every possible heartfelt consolation. There were the usual suspects, "He's in a better place" or "I know this is hard but . . ." However, it was after overhearing "But she's young" the second time that my blood began to boil. I'm young?! I could typically tell by the tone that this was meant to be a positive statement to remind me of a light at the end of this tunnel. What light? My world was dark, and though yes, I figured somehow by the grace of God, I would go on, I knew the tunnel was to be very long, and some lights in my future might never shine.

She's young. Is grief easier for the young? I know from past experiences and even watching my nieces mourn the loss of their Uncle Dusty, that yes, children somehow have an amazing resiliency after tragedy. I think this is where the "faith of a child" is perhaps best demonstrated. They feel loss deeply, no doubt, but they are able to understand and accept eternal hope as a fact and not a possibility. I, however, was not a child. I would be thirty in less than a year, and though I admired and aspired for the faith of a child, especially in this, I found that it was not just my aged skin that lacked buoyancy but my bruised spirit as well. Or by my youth were they inferring that because Dustin and I had not had the luxury of growing old together, I could not possibly know or feel grief as deeply as my elder counterparts—the ones who'd raised children, built homes, traveled miles, and embraced each other's wrinkles with the same smiles that produced them. Those milestones and the memories were unknown to me. I would argue that in this instance, perhaps the young widow feels twice the agony, once for the life lost and then for the one never to come—the death of a dream.

She's young. I get it. What they meant by "she's young" is that I had plenty of years ahead of me to start a new life. They assumed that I would marry again and have children and all would be well again. If only it was that simple. They were only partially to blame for their insensitivity, or should I say, untimely remarks. They clearly did not understand the dream. It was not about checking off life boxes: husband—check! Baby—check! No, this was a play I began writing the day I fell in love with the man who would be my husband, and the scenes and characters weren't supposed to be substituted by any understudy, though the plot seemed universal.

One Sunday not long after Dustin had passed, I watched my nieces playing with one of the church babies. The little girl was about six months old at the time and was always decked out in the cutest outfits with bows as big as her head. She was a charmer no doubt, but watching the girls giggle with her and swing her in the air cut deeply. When Dustin and I attended family dinners, I would catch myself daydreaming of the day when everyone would gather around our little bundle of joy and Ooo and Ahh because all the other grandkids were well passed the diaper stage. I pictured our nieces taking him or her all around and beaming with pride as would Grammy and Papa and aunts and uncles. I thought about it often, but then watched someone else's baby get that honor. I think that's when the burning began as I watched my dreams play out in the lives of others.

There were two other young couples in the church who'd married shortly after us. I would stare at them sometimes when they weren't looking, wondering how their lives would play out, fascinated that somehow they'd avoided drawing the short straw and were coasting on the usual first-year bliss. What was that even like? Within a year of marriage, both were expecting their first child. Of course they were. Though we were all relatively the same ages, I felt old next to them, as if I'd already lived a lifetime. I hear the term "widow," and I subconsciously associate it with gray hair and antique wedding rings on knobby fingers. Even after multiple years, the title still seems alien to me, but it's the box I now check.

In my earlier—and more bitter—days of grieving, I made mental notes of all the feeble offerings of comfort doled out through empty and misplaced words. I would write a book about that, I thought, an exposé on all the ridiculousness people throw at those in mourning, the endless Band-Aids of words and the internal bleeding that won't stop. To their "she's young" comments, I thought, *I'll show them!* But show them what? Explain how? And if I couldn't explain my feelings, then could I really hold them accountable for their ignorance?

I find it a tragic irony that despite my journey, I still falter in offering condolences and, on occasion, may have caused ears to bleed needlessly. I've shuffled through many receiving lines since Dustin's death, looked into many hollow faces, and felt the same loss for words, and in sheer panic reverted to the old faithfuls. Some have been permanently banned from my vocabulary, but I sadly still find myself occasionally giving out Band-Aids.

I understood very early on that there is no manual for grief—neither for those experiencing it or those trying to console it. As the mourner, you volley back and forth between wanting silence and needing to talk, and navigating those waters from an outsider's perspective can be daunting. As much as I hoped grace would be given to me in my crazy moments, I realized I must also extend grace to those who said the wrong thing at the wrong time or never said anything at all.

Dustin's and my time together was brief, and yes, we were relatively young. I have now spent more years mourning his loss than knowing him. However, I eventually chose to believe that those who glorified my youth in the face of tragedy did so not as a reproach to me or our love but in the spirit of hope for a time of healing and restoration to come, a time of new beginnings that I both long for and fear.

5

Ambulance Chasers. Though the expression was new to me at the time, I was surprised at how perfectly it captured the gall of many a sympathetic onlooker to our tragedy. An Ambulance Chaser is someone who has a magnetic draw to crises, more out of a desire to be "in the know" than generosity of spirit. My mom taught me the term after we were introduced to so many that first week as the sirens echoed their way through circles of friends, family, church members, and work colleagues. In all fairness, there were many strangers who were drawn to our story out of sincere sadness and with a genuine desire to help. I confess that my recollections of the ambulance chasers is somewhat skewed by my emotional volatility at that time.

One incident in particular nearly sent me into full orbit. Suffice it to say, an intimate family moment was violated by an unwanted, albeit well-intentioned, guest. As we stood discussing very personal memories, I felt rage surge within me as this virtual outsider sat front-and-center to our family's private grief. How dare they hear these stories and nod sympathetically, soaking in details I assumed they would share over coffee with other "sympathizers?" I kept my head down, diverted from their gaze, certain my eyes would give me away. I loathed their presence, and every minute they loitered stretched on like an hour.

In the safety of our car, I unloaded on my mom. I spewed horrible thoughts churned from a boiling anger that seemed to ignite on a whim in those days. I magnified the lack of consideration to a moral injustice. I had planned to return home that night to work on my letter to Dustin, the one I would read at the memorial, but my state of fury would not lend to the appropriate sentiments I wished to convey. I could, however, write a colorful diatribe on my new term of the day. Ambulance chasers—yes, they were everywhere.

I sat isolated in my bedroom, staring at the computer screen, when my friend called to discuss the program for the memorial. She'd been working on the format and wanted my opinion on the first draft. I opened the attachment to find a large picture of Dustin's beautiful face smiling back at me, and I lost it.

"No, it's too big." I said.

"What's too big?" she said.

"His picture; they don't get to see him. They don't all get to have his picture!" I said.

"Ok . . ." she said. "They?"

"Yes, them! The people at the service." I snapped.

"Hmm . . . alright; can I ask why?" she asked cautiously.

I vented passionately about the incident earlier that evening, stoking the fire again. I pictured this sea of onlookers in the sanctuary, a sea of ambulance chasers, spectators. I might not be able to bar them from the doors, but they would not leave with a tangible token of his life. They didn't deserve it. I spoke with the conviction of a madwoman frantically waving her weapon of choice to prove a point and mental instability. I was standing on the ledge, shouting out nonsense on the phone, while my friend negotiated calmly for me to crawl back through the window and rejoin the rest of the world. Though she questioned my motives, she never belittled the crazy. She let it breathe fire and gradually burn out.

"So, no picture," I said.

"Ok, well, while I understand your frustration, I still think a picture of him would be nice. The majority of people attending his service are people who loved him dearly, who love you and his family. Let them see him. It will be ok," she said.

I surrendered, and the next day I felt like a complete fool. I don't drink, but I felt the remorse of the morning after a drunken escapade. I called my friend to apologize, already knowing it wasn't necessary, but thankful for her beyond words. His picture did grace the cover of the program. He was handsome with his quirky smirk and piercing eyes. It was the perfect picture of him, and in the end, I was happy to share it, with ambulance chasers and all.

I marvel at my attempts to adapt to societal norms despite feeling like a crazy person inside. It's one aspect of grief I feel is sometimes overlooked—the constant state of disorientation and just plain crazy that seems to swallow the once-sane. I'm not talking about random outbursts of tears; those moments I think can easily be explained. No, I'm referring to the strange thoughts that plague the mind of the griever and occasionally lead to even stranger actions as exemplified by my ambulance chaser soapbox. To be clear, I'm not speaking to any form of clinical mental breakdown that can certainly happen as a result of tragedy but rather the moments of subtitle crazy that leave one frustrated and feeling foolish. I have no answers or solutions, but sometimes the validation that you're not alone in your occasional "crazy" can be freeing.

Unfortunately, the crazy was not confined to the week of the memorial. It would lie dormant for a time and then rear its ugly head most inconveniently. I tried to keep it contained but found it had a mind of its own.

Growing up, my family always had cats. In fact, for most of my childhood we had four cats, all indoors and spoiled rotten. In my baby album, there's countless pictures of me holding any one of them hostage by the neck as the rest of their bodies dangled helplessly. My grandmother had the fattest of cats that she could barely carry up the stairs, and their lovely San Diego home was decorated with artistic feline accents. One of my favorite memories with her is of the two of us sitting at her piano while she played "Memories" from the musical *CATS. Of course.* My feet swung in the air with each crescendo as I tried to join her in singing what lyrics I could pick up at the age of eight.

Naturally, there was no fighting the genetic disposition; I was born to be a cat person.

My first job after college required a great deal of travel, so owning a pet would just be cruel for an animal forced to spend most of its days in an empty apartment. When Dustin and I met, neither of us had pets, and he was certainly not in favor of our getting a cat. He only had dogs growing up and was firmly in that camp. He bought into the propaganda that cats were temperamental and mean; it didn't help that he was also allergic. Our for-better-or-worse vows forced me to concede to a feline-free life.

I can't recall at what point we started entertaining the notion of getting a pet—let alone a cat—but sure enough, I gradually swayed his resolve. One of our friends at church mentioned she had a co-worker giving away kittens, and Dustin suggested we at least check them out. Turns out he was only mildly allergic, and our current lifestyle wouldn't really accommodate a boisterous puppy.

"But you don't like cats," I said.

"But you do," he said. *Ah, love.*

We were headed out of town that weekend but planned to pick up the newest addition to the family on our way home. Our friend sent pictures of the little calico kitten, and we passed the time on the road debating names. We arrived at the house to be greeted by a box full of kittens, and while I quickly identified our kitten, a little, fuzzy ball of orange and white fur bounded up towards my lap. He was irresistibly cute, but we were there for ONE kitten. I held the calico while Dustin wrestled with other. I was noticeably torn, but I felt we'd already committed to the little girl. We couldn't leave her behind now.

"Let's get them both!" he said decidedly with a twinkle in his eye.

"We can't get TWO kittens! Are you crazy?" I said, feeling a match brewing between our spontaneous and practical natures. I listed out all the logical reasons why this would not be a good idea—the cost of getting two cats fixed, let alone all their shots, the litter box for two cats in a small apartment with no utility room, and last but certainly not least, the pet deposit. He was unfazed.

"Oh, we'll make it work; it will be fun. They'll keep each other company," he said.

Ten minutes later, we left the house with a box of, not one, but two kittens, and the role reversal began. I fretted the entire drive back about what we'd just gotten ourselves into while he made a mental list of the supplies he needed to pick up for the kids. It was like going to the obstetrician planning to see one baby, only to have the sonogram reveal twins! And it was one of the best decisions we'd ever made . . . and by we, I mean *he*.

Brother and sister became the best of companions and even slept encircled in each other's embrace in their little bed. We named them Tyler and Izze (pronounced Izzy), and each had a host of other nicknames. In a matter of weeks, *we* were domesticated and found our conversations revolved around what new trick the kitties learned. Naturally, I was thrilled to have cats again, but my enthusiasm paled in comparison to Dustin's. Even his family was shocked and amused by the endless pictures he'd post on social media of "the kids." He would go to the store to get litter and return with endless treats and accessories. I may have been the more seasoned cat person, but I was never one to shower my pets with endless collars, toys, and beds. Growing up, we provided the basics and lots of love, and they were just fine. Tyler and Izze, however, reaped the blessings of a doting dad while mom balked at the store receipts.

It was his fascination with the cats that led to a resurgence of the crazy in me that first summer. Those who have pets will understand they are very sensitive to an upset in the balance of the home, much like children. They can sense when something is off or someone is absent. I remember in those first weeks, Izze would sometimes sit by the front door, just waiting. She and Dustin had a special bond, and I could tell she missed him greatly. One night she curled up right next to me in bed, her head turned facing mine as if to say, "We'll get through this together, you and me." I struggled to help them adjust, which in itself seemed a little bizarre, but their sadness reminded me of my own and our broken family.

It was an uneventful Friday that quickly became eventful when I realized it was May 3, and the kitties were officially one year old. *What mom forgets her kids' birthday?!* Again, had their birthday occurred under normal circumstances, it might have been marked by a little tuna in their food dish and some Happy Birthday snuggles, but Dustin turned the world of cat ownership upside-down. I would've argued against it, but ultimately, he'd go out for something small and come back with a giant contraption for them to explore. I could picture him pouring over instructions, or not, and assembling their gift while they sniffed, and I stood in the background shaking my head.

But there were no gifts, not even any tuna for their bowl, because I'd completely forgotten. I jumped off the couch with no plan but overwhelmed by an urgent sense of guilt. I had to make this right. I grabbed my purse and sped to the nearest store and paced up and down the pet aisles. *Ok, the first birthday is a big deal, so I need to find something special for them, something Dustin would've picked.* My wallet was drawn to the catnip mice. *This is not the time to be cheap! You're always the cheap one.* And there it was—a mini bungalow with hidden compartments, scratching post, dangling toy, and top lookout perch. It was very cool, and it was $30. I'd never spent so much on a pet, not for a toy. I knew good and well that the kittens were just as content scratching the side of our couch as they would be this contraption, but it was their birthday, their first without Dustin. *Because animals know when it's their birthday.*

I made the 911 call to Jaci because I was going to need to be coached through this.

"So I really need your help. It's the kitties' birthday, and I forgot!" I said. I was a little too out of breath for the truly non-event that was taking place. I was hyperventilating in a store aisle over cat things; I'd reached a whole new low.

"Ok . . . go on," she said, stalling I'm sure for time to come up with a response to the peculiar conversation about to ensue.

I went through my entire logic behind celebrating the birthday and needing to do something special, something worthy of Dustin. I couldn't let him down, but there was the issue of the $30 cat toy and my frugality. I knew I called the right person because Jaci's thriftiness is ten to my one, so she would tell me straight. I love her for many reasons, but her response on that night is one I cherish the most.

"Well of course you must buy it! It's their birthday after all," she said with great conviction. "And this is the first without Dustin. Yes, spend the $30 and throw something extra in while you're at it." *Now she was talking crazy!*

Mind you, Jaci is not a pet person. She owns them but is more of a landlord than a lover. She tolerates fur but cuddles minimally. She does NOT spend money on pets, but she does love her friend. She was able to filter through my crazy rant to help me find an outlet to ease the loneliness of that night and honor Dustin in a small, but meaningful way.

I tearfully thanked her for answering my SOS and made my way to the register. I left triumphant and excited to show Tyler and Izze their new toy. The rest of the evening was spent with plastic parts strewn across the carpet while I fiddled through directions, a labor of love indeed. When it was assembled, I couldn't have been more proud, and to highlight the craziness of the night, I took a video of the cats exploring it for the first time. And . . . I posted it on Facebook. I was officially the crazy cat lady, and I didn't care.

6

When I was younger, my dad, who I call Papa, was in charge of checking my math homework. In hopes that his corrections would lead to lessons learned, he would come up with names for my alter-egos who kept making errors. Careless Carla and Paula Procrastinator made the most appearances on home-work night. I blame my mom, an English teacher, for my math deficiencies, but my penchant for procrastination is all Papa. Thankfully, they both instilled a strong work ethic in my broth-er and me, but Paula still makes occasional appearances in my adult life as well. I was a week away from moving out of our apartment, and I was putting off the inevitable.

I came home from a work event, walked straight to the bed-room, and shut the door, collapsing on the bed in darkness. I was holding on tightly because I knew I was about to have to let some of our life go, and it made me miss him greatly. I wanted him to be there so badly, to hold me in the night and calm my fears. Instead, I clung to his pillow and drenched it with tears.

The move was a good thing. Our friends were in the military and facing a short deployment that didn't warrant finding renters. They offered their home to me as a change of scenery while they were away. They said I would be doing them a great favor by staying in the house, but it was really I who reaped the blessing. Though the thought of leaving the only home we'd ever known was hard, I knew deep down I needed a different environment to jump-start my healing. Plus, the move would give me time to look for a place of my own and not feel rushed. It was a good thing, and Dustin would be pleased. I was grateful for friends who stepped up to take care of me in those days, and there were many. I agreed to the arrangement but asked for some time. They were leaving only two months after his passing, and I couldn't wrap my head around a move like that so soon. Yes, it was time to leave the apartment, but not before I'd said my good-byes.

I thought the month of June would be long enough—that I'd leisurely pack and spend hours recounting memories. There was time for that, but I was not making much progress. With a week left to go, I found myself too tired for the task ahead. I had reached the road block in packing that Dustin was all too familiar with after the move from my apartment to the one we shared after we were married. I'm not a fan of change—a slow-mover and sentimental—which made a move of this nature almost impossible. I ached for him in a whole new way. Who knew there were so many degrees of pain?

I was re-reading *The Shack* at the time. *Misery loves company.* I hadn't read very far, but I understood The Great Sadness all too well.

The Great Sadness had draped itself around Mack's shoulders like some invisible but almost tangible heavy guilt. The weight of its presence dulled his eyes and stooped his shoulders. Even his efforts to shake it off were exhausting, as if his arms were sewn into its bleak folds of despair, and he had somehow become part of it. He ate, worked, loved, dreamed and played in this garment of heaviness, weighed down as if he were wearing a leaden bathrobe—trudging daily through the murky despondency that sucked the color of everything.[1]

Life lacked color, and now our apartment lacked it as well with all the paintings taken down from the walls. Without his presence, the rooms were hollow chambers, and the grief felt claustrophobic. I'd aimlessly move from room to room picking up random objects here and there only to move them to another room where they sat orphaned in piles. I received many offers of help, but I declined every one of them. I felt strangely possessive of our home and barred all intruders from our space. I had to do this alone.

I had one weekend before my parents arrived, and I'd promised them some modicum of productivity since we would have only one weekend to move everything. I planned to hole myself up in the apartment and surrender to the sadness. Books and dishes could be easily boxed up, but clothes . . . clothes that he'd worn and everyday items he touched . . . those would be handled with ceremonial reverence, bathed in tears.

I packed at the pace of a five-year-old who starts to put her toys away but then becomes distracted by them and wants to play. I was distracted by everything because everything had a story, and I desperately wanted to play pretend. Pretend I was folding endless undershirts because it was laundry day and not because they were no longer needed. I had multiple piles—the clothes I would give to his brother and father, clothes to be donated and the clothes I would keep because I just couldn't part with them, not yet. Items like the shirts that had special significance and the pairs of Converse that were so quintessentially Dustin fell into that category. In fact, for our wedding, I'd custom designed a pair for him to wear with his tuxedo. One of my favorite pictures from our reception is of him dancing with his mom. The photographer zoomed in for a shot of her pale pink high heels keeping in step with his gray Converse. I kept one shoe and gave her the other.

I tried to be cognizant of fact that his family would want some of his things as well, and though they were not invited to the packing party, I made sure to remember them as I sorted. I figured some of the shirts might even still fit his brother or father, and I could imagine it might be comforting for them to have something of his they could keep close, or even wear if they felt so inclined. It's an unsettling reality to be shopping in your husband's closet for tokens to give to loved ones.

Not everything in the apartment had sentimental value. Sometimes after death, any item owned by that person is almost idolized and preserved as though their memory was tied to the object's existence. I, on the other hand, was quite eager to dispose of some of our collections—the food dehydrator being one of them. I remember the day we became the new owners of this giant, multilayered orb of food preservation. I had just left for work when Dustin called to ask me if I'd noticed the apartment garage sale that was going on by the front gate. I had, and as I drove past the tables of what I viewed as junk, I prayed somehow Dustin would not notice. It was a pointless prayer. He was drawn to those tables like a moth to the flame, and he returned with the food dehydrator, among other things. It was never used; I knew it wouldn't be. We just shifted it around from time to time when we needed space. No, I would not be sad to part ways with it, and I felt that was a good sign of sanity. I determined that in packing, sorting, and decluttering I would not be bound by obligation but meaning only. Our lives were for a time being packed up in boxes to be stored till a new life began.

In our short time together, we'd acquired our own décor and made a series of changes here and there to make our apartment feel like home. We laughed. We loved. We argued and made up. We were just beginning. I felt like in one year we lived a small lifetime striving to make good on every vow. You just can't process all those memories in a weekend, but I tried. I buried my face in his clothes searching for his scent. I clutched them and wept. I sat with each piece like an old friend, begging it to tell me "remember when" stories so I wouldn't forget. I kept the curtains closed and mourned him deeply in those seventy-two hours.

There was one box in particular left to pack. It would not fit much in the way of belongings, but it became a treasure chest of memories. In the weeks leading up to moving day, I became very anxious. *As if I needed another excuse to procrastinate.* I second guessed my decision on more than one occasion, wondering if it was too soon. It had only been a couple of months since his death, and what if I closed the door prematurely on a time of therapeutic reflection prompted by our space and things? Once it was all packed up, there would be no going back. Oh sure, I could look at old photos and mementos, but I would never again occupy the rooms where we'd lived our married life. Never is a desolate word. It immediately sends you backpedaling.

Dustin no longer resided at that address, but I doubted the longevity of his memories outside those apartment walls. I felt like I needed a signal, a green light to proceed, and I needed it to come from him. If he could write it in a letter, that would be ideal; then I could have the letter to keep with me and reread when I felt unsteady. I mean if there was a host of angels in heaven to welcome him when he went home, surely one of them could moonlight as a carrier pigeon for the grieving left behind. I suppose that was the crazy coming out, but it stemmed from very real fears.

Just in time, a package was delivered with no return address on a day of brooding apprehension. There was no letter or note, only a box within the box. It was small, 5x7, three inches tall, and there was an opening in the lid for a picture. Above the picture window was engraved *Our Home* with our address engraved below. I stared at it awe struck and a little spooked to be quite honest. *Could it be? Nah . . .* Still, I brushed my fingers over the engraving lost in thought. Our home. In that solemn moment, I cried for what was lost and what had been found—the release to go.

I chose to fill the box with little things that would hopefully one day remind me of our quirky life in that apartment. To someone else, it would be a pretty box filled with random, seemingly unrelated items. I opened this time capsule recently and found randomness indeed: lip balm, mini prep bowls, a bottle cap, cat collars, a bamboo stem, and on and on. Lip balm was a constant pocket companion of Dustin's. The mini prep bowls—*and I mean mini*—were used to siphon off spices and other small portioned ingredients. The bottle cap was from our favorite drink, which became our cat's namesake. The cat collars were picked by him, though I was the "cat person." The stem was from our first indoor plant. My family never had indoor plants because it was basically decorative cat food, so the concept was foreign to me. When Dustin transplanted his little bamboo plant into a pot for the living room, he took a dramatic breath and exhaled loudly saying, "Finally, we have something living in this place!" *Clearly, the two humans didn't count.*

I later found out the mysterious gift was sent by a very thoughtful friend who didn't think about including a note. Maybe I was meant to receive it that way. It forced me out of my funk and prompted a burst of inspired energy. I had to find creative ways to hide clues in the box that would serve as reminders of our life for the future me. Life in Our Home.

I had enough sense to hire movers to take all of our furniture and boxes to the storage unit—best money I ever spent. Since I'd become obsessed with my privacy when it came to the move, it was up to my parents and me to get everything done. I was thankful the movers were incredibly efficient, too efficient. I was still frantically throwing stuff in boxes while they were hauling off dressers and beds in record time. It was late that night when we moved the last of my clothes and personal items to my temporary residence. We drove like zombies on the verge of madness listening to my two cats scream and yowl as if they were being tortured in their crates.

It would take me a couple years to unpack all that had been stuffed away, to include *Our Home* box. I learned there were ways I could keep pieces of Dustin throughout my new home, unbeknownst to visitors. I liked it that way. It was a way I could keep him close without putting my grief on display. They were secret treasures, and we had an understanding that we would always remember him regardless of how quickly the world moved on around us.

7

It was a normal Wednesday of little significance. I had survived the weekend of the move and was now getting my footing again. Our apartment was empty except for a few bags of clothes, and after work, I planned to stop by to pick up the last of it and say good-bye to our home. I was initially quite motivated, needing for this step to be finished, but as I neared our gates, I became mindful that this was the last time I'd be driving through them. I'd asked his best friend to meet me. I had some things of Dustin's to give him, and he was also going to take the remainder of Dustin's clothes to a local men's rehabilitation facility. I knew Dustin would've wanted me to do that, so I was pleased with the plan, just not the finality of it all. After the exchanges had been made, and we said our goodbyes for the night, I turned the key in the lock. Click. It was no longer ours, and I drove away in silence.

A weary me later arrived at church that evening for midweek Bible study. I sat in my seat and listened dutifully, tired but relieved that the apartment key had been turned in, and I never had to go back. Once our class was over, I left the room only to hear familiar laughter down the hall. I say laughter because one does not run into my father-in-law without the accompaniment of laughter. He's either telling jokes or making them up on the fly, but regardless, he is a genuine delight. My in-laws are salt-of-the-earth people who love freely and serve endlessly. They are also two of the most adventurous people I know, and I am incredibly blessed to have been welcomed into their hearts from the very beginning.

Despite his jovial temperament that evening, I knew it was hard for him to walk the halls of our church. It must have taken great effort for him to be there, let alone be pleasant. Memories of Dustin in that place were a heavy burden for him, though the same halls comforted me. I took a deep breath summoning my last ounce of enthusiasm for the day and stepped into the pastor's office where he waited with arms outstretched for a hug, and I froze. Before me stood my sweet father-in-law dressed in one of Dustin's polo shirts. It took everything in me to carry on the conversation that ensued. I heard his words and nodded while the shirt spun around in my head. Not days earlier, I'd wept over that shirt as I removed it from our dresser and placed it in a bag. I had no doubt his dad might wear one from time to time. I'd hoped he would if it would bring him comfort, and in retrospect, it likely gave him the little bit of courage he needed to face friends in a place less familiar without Dustin. I just was not ready for it that night.

There was no avoiding our exchange and certainly no way he could've known the previous events of the day—nor could I have known the sadness that must have swallowed him when he removed the shirt from the bag. We both longed for Dustin, and having just spent a weekend of grasping at the tangible, I conceded it was his turn. I grieved as a wife. I didn't know what it was to grieve as a parent, though somehow I knew it must be the ultimate loss. I don't think any of us knew how to navigate the road we were on; we just trudged it as best as we could.

Because I was emotionally and physically exhausted, the reality of what faced me stirred emotions I had not the strength to contain. I think we discussed celebrating my birthday later that week. I was torn between loving him dearly and wanting to flee the scene. At the sound of my mother-in-law's voice down the hall, he promptly hugged me and left with the promise of a birthday dinner in my future.

The second he turned the corner, I gasped as if I'd been holding my breath underwater, and the dam burst. I started to cry audibly and shake, neither of which I did in public if I could at all help it. This night, I could not. My pastor quickly assessed the scene and yelled for the young boys playing games in the corner of his office to leave. I felt their wide-eyes, and I rolled towards the wall to hide my face and tears while they were ushered out of the room. I begged the wall to swallow me up so I didn't have to see any more faces. I was shocked and embarrassed by my unusual response and my lack of ability to control it.

His wife came in quickly after with eyes of concern and arms to hold me till the shaking stopped. I felt for her and others of our friends who now had to navigate the grief of our entire family, as we went to the same church and all needed support. I composed myself eventually and quickly exited the building so I could put myself to bed and out of my misery. The next day, all was well as if it had never happened. That's the nature of triggers. They are like live mines waiting to explode at the first misstep, but after the commotion, silence. I was about to learn firsthand that I could not only experience them but set them off as well.

As promised, the family gathered for my birthday dinner later that week. I met the rest of the clan at the restaurant after work, and I appreciated the family's efforts to be celebratory though that year I'd just as soon taken a pass. I was having a good day that day. They came more frequently with every passing month. The good days were marked by smiles, genuine ambition for life, and a gentle missing of him that still allowed for functioning. It had been the first good day in a while, so I relished it and found myself being rather chatty at dinner.

"How are you doing, sissy?" My mother-in-law asked. She understood the heaviness of the move and is always thinking of others above herself.

I responded with an upbeat tone that may have surprised her, and I rattled off the details of the recent days since the move with ease. Again, it was a good day, and you eventually learn to just embrace those as they come. However, in my chattiness, I think I initially missed the nonverbal cues of her tired eyes and slow-coming smiles, or else I might have been more cautious with my updates.

"Oh and I was able to donate the rest of Dustin's clothes . . . " I blabbed proudly about finding a way for his clothes to be of use to others in need since I knew, and figured she did too, that he would've wanted it that way. Yet my speech slowed, and I quickly wrapped up the conversation when I saw a brief flicker across her eyes that spoke a warning to me. It was not a harsh look by any means. What I saw was a stab of pain, as if I'd pricked her with a needle. In a flash it was gone, but I learned much in those seconds. I hadn't thought about how the news of her son's clothes being divvied out would hit her ears. I'd thought only of myself and not of a mother grieving the baby she birthed and the child she raised into a man, the man who called her "Mama" even in his twenties.

I had assumed it was a good day for her as well, but instead, I may have been the very trigger that ruined an otherwise pleasant meal. I opened cards, and we exchanged pleasantries for a little while longer. I carried more from the restaurant than just my gifts that night. I carried a twinge of guilt and a life lesson learned.

Grief is like weight. We all gain it after overindulging for extended periods of time, but we carry it differently depending on our body shape. On some, it is more noticeable than others, and then there are those with the frames of magicians where the weight seems to completely disappear. But it's there. It's there for all of us, and it weighs upon us whether we verbalize it or not. It is as unique as a fingerprint and just as hard to decipher. There are no microscopes into the soul, which invariably lead to ill-timed outbursts, unintentional offenses, and thoughtless oversights. This was not a one-woman show. We'd all loved Dustin, and we all shared ownership in his memory as wife, mother, father, sister, brother, uncle, and in-laws. There were many characters to this tragedy, and we all played our parts differently.

I learned over time how to be true to myself while also giving consideration for the feelings of those around me. I could not expect them to walk my road, but I had to allow them to journey theirs. I had to be patient with their expressions of grief when they differed from mine. Patience meant the absence of judgment and question, and it had been extended to me on many occasions. We were a family. Ultimately, we would heal more completely if we learned to support each other, and support each other we have, to this very day.

Healing

8

We've all been there at least once in our childhood—the slumber party that goes horribly wrong. Whether it was your very first, a time the company was questionable, or just an off night—in that moment all you can think of is going home where it is safe. It's that one night when no amount of pillow fights, girly movies, or junk food smorgasbords can take the edge off. You try to play it cool with your friends all the while casting furtive glances at the clock only to realize it's not even midnight, and you have eight more hours before you can be picked up without attracting suspicion. Finally, in desperation, you sneak down the stairs to the phone in the kitchen and hide beneath the counter as you make your clandestine phone call for an immediate extraction. You simply cannot stand the suffocation of your surroundings any longer, and your brave façade is giving way to tears. At twenty-eight years of age, miles away from home, I regressed to my eight-year-old, slumber-party self and sneaked a tearful phone call to my mom. I wanted to come home.

You laugh—maybe because you can relate or because of the irony of a grown woman questioning her ability to function beyond that of a child—and yet after a tragic loss, a child you become. It's often said that grief ages you. I'm sure I will have the wrinkles and gray hairs to show for it later, but I would also argue that grief rewinds the hands of time till your body still looks every bit the grown-up but your mind and heart are that of a child. You feel small inside, at times helpless, and when life backs you into a corner of the unfamiliar, you may lash out. But deep down you strangely long for your favorite blanket, chocolate chip cookies, and Mommy's lap.

I was in Kentucky visiting a friend for Memorial Day weekend. This friend had moved back to Kentucky with her husband after his service at Fort Hood was complete, and though we'd only worked together for three years at most, we'd remained very close. It had been my turn to visit for quite some time, but I was too busy falling in love and getting married to be able to journey to the Blue Grass state.

Shortly after Dustin's memorial, I knew I'd need intermittent escapes, and visiting Devon in Kentucky seemed like a good plan for the Memorial Day holiday. Though I was genuinely looking forward to the trip and seeing an old friend, my heart rate began to rise as the plane neared its final destination. I've been fortunate to have traveled to many destinations throughout my life and enjoy it immensely, so I was surprised by this sense of legitimate panic ensuing on what otherwise would've been a very uneventful flight. Once off the plane, the sensation only grew and was then accompanied by a rather large lump in my throat and mist in my eyes. I called my mom (first call). Of course she was bubbly on the other end and enthusiastic about my trip but quickly surmised I was not feeling the same way.

"What if I can't do this?" I said.

My own words were strange to me, and even as my heart pleaded for reassurance, my mind was baffled by the conversation. What was so difficult about visiting a friend? I'd spent my early twenties jetting all over the country to visit friends without batting an eye, but that evening in the Louisville airport, I realized I was not that same girl. Some behaviors and confidences would have to be relearned. Though I had ventured out since Dustin's passing on a number of occasions, I always had the safety of my apartment to return to afterwards. When an event or gathering got too intense, I could leave early or hang in for the final minutes knowing at least I could go home and cry or collapse in my bed. This was different. For the first time in two months, running home was not an option, and that made me nervous. Praise God for wise mothers who know instinctively what to say. She gave the gentle pep talk I needed to leave the terminal without tears.

The next day, Devon and I ventured off to begin sightseeing and had a great time. The countryside was beautiful and lush with rich history. I was captivated by the scenery and content just to look out the window in awe. We took a break from being tourists to shop a bit, and while she was looking at maternity bargains, I pretended to look at jewelry in another section. Within minutes I was on my cell phone, hurriedly dialing mom (second call). Initially, I intended to put her mind at ease after the airport SOS, but I couldn't tell if I was convincing her or myself that I was having a good time. I ducked in and out of rows of tops and dresses trying to hide the fact that I was on the phone with my mom on what was supposed to be a girl's weekend. I didn't want my friend to feel like she wasn't being a good host, so every time she stepped out of the dressing room to show me a new outfit, I shoved mom in my pocket, gave a thumbs up or down to the outfit in question, and then returned to my conversation when the dressing room door was closed. This act was repeated at least three more times.

What I realized over the course of the clandestine conversation was that I truly was having a good time, and that was the problem. I did thoroughly enjoy every farm we drove past and little town we strolled through, but the rush of the scenic beauty was accompanied by a growing pit in my stomach. I was on vacation, and Dustin was not there with me. Even worse, I could not pick up the phone and share with him my enthusiasm, and he would not be at the apartment to welcome me home when I returned, ready to hear the stories of my adventures. There would be no vacations for us. The reality hit me hard at the worst of times, and I wondered if the rest of trip would be just as heavy.

Although initially there were no set plans for the evening, plans quickly found us. One of Devon's friends suggested a girlfriends' reunion between friends who had once been a part of a Bible study group. Of course Devon was not about to commit me to anything outside of my now strangely-limited comfort zone, so I emphatically waved my arms in support while she was on the phone.

I've never been one to say "No." It's one of the smallest words in the dictionary, and yet for me quite possibly the hardest to say! Almost immediately after I'd given my then-sincere vote of approval, I began to second-guess myself. *What have I just committed to?* I was not worried about the company per se. These were women Devon had often shared about, and on a normal day, or should I say two months ago, I would've joined right in, no reservations. But they weren't just women; they were wives —happily married, some with kids, some without, but all with futures . . . and husbands. *What would I talk about? How will it feel?*

I didn't immediately shift in reverse, but I started slowly backpedaling. *Did these women even know?* In social situations, it's truly awkward when someone learns of your tragedy for the first time. It's not so much because you're forced to verbalize the painful reality, as much as the obvious discomfort and foot-in-mouth anguish you see on the other person's face as they squirm uncontrollably or stand frozen in shock. Suddenly, you find yourself consoling Foot-in-Mouth with, "Oh no, please don't feel bad; you didn't know" and quickly trying to lighten the mood. Thankfully, these are usually hit-and-run instances, but at a dinner table surrounded by searching faces . . . *Oh, no.*

I could already see Devon's excitement, and I wasn't about

to spoil the party. I voiced my concerns and asked her to make sure everyone knew about Dustin prior to our arrival. It would really be better all around. She wholeheartedly agreed and was even sweet enough to offer me one last out. I declined, and she promised it wouldn't be a marathon evening. We'd eat. We'd chat. We'd go home (with dessert).

It was a good plan, but even as I was calming to the idea of the night out, I still overheard the conversation on the phone. Apparently her friend hadn't heard the news. *Great.* In an effort to be brief and get back to her company, Devon quickly summarized my hell in two minutes. I should've been grateful at her swift approach. Instead, my stomach flipped, and the tears started to form. In minutes, I was outside on the steps after having made some excuse about needing to call someone about something. I called my mom (third call), and I cried. On the steps of a nondescript Lexington apartment, I cried like a little girl and wanted to go home.

From day one of this tragedy, God had supernaturally infused my mom with a well-spring of wisdom. I don't know how she did it, but she coaxed me back from the railing and reminded me of what was true. No one was being insensitive to my plight, and I wasn't rushing out prematurely. It was just life, and as much as I was adjusting, everyone else around me was too. The one thing I could be sure of was that I was loved by my friend, and God was with me. They'd both be by my side no matter what the night held. And as it happened, the night held pleasant surprises of laughter, light conversation, and VERY good food. I quickly learned that five women who'd known me for two hours loved me as if they'd known me for years. My heart was blessed and in awe. Though I might never see them again, somehow I knew they'd be praying for me for years to come.

Finally, after a full day out and about, it was time to head back to the apartment—an apartment, I might add, with only one bedroom. Though certainly not uncommon for a young couple, I'd given myself quite the pep talk the night before when I learned there would be no escape bedroom for when I was tired, emotionally and/or physically, although I was sure to play it off as sleep deprivation. You see, that was part of the panic intervention from Mom at the airport—"When you feel overwhelmed, just excuse yourself to the guest room and rest; Devon will understand." *Um, what's Plan C?* In truth, I slept rather well the first night and had come to accept that a living room futon was a small price to pay for good company. Sometimes the escape you need is not hidden behind four walls but in the arms of a dear friend.

9

Despite the torrential upheaval in my spirit, I continued to attend church regularly. Church has always been a second home to me, and it was my church family who propped me up in those early days. To be MIA for too long would signal the alarms I tried to keep at bay. It's strange how you want people to be mindful of your pain and teetering state, but you are also desperately trying to be your old self (whoever that was) to establish some sense of normalcy (whatever that is). Sunday morning worship was both a welcome reprieve and an awkward date with the Man I'd both clung to and avoided since March 21, 2011.

In our church sanctuary, the lights are typically dimmed during the first part of the service while we sing the worship songs projected on the screen and led by the band. The darkness is like a comforting cloak that makes you invisible. You can sing and cry without fear of being noticed. You are in the middle of a crowd, yet alone in your thoughts. I liked the crowd—I was not ready to be alone with Him in this setting. At these times, it was a love/hate relationship. Like a child, I wanted to run into the open arms awaiting me, yet those arms had allowed Dustin's death. On this day, I stared those arms down while crossing my own. I dutifully sang the words of familiar choruses. I would sing, but I could not praise. He asked too much.

One, two, three songs. By my account, we were nearing the end of worship time. I was almost home free, until the notes of the final song were strummed on the guitar, *I Love You Lord.* I knew the verses by heart, a classic from my childhood, though the composition was different. The familiar words began to draw me in, begging the question—did I still love Him? After all that had happened and the wreckage of my present life, did I still love Him the same? *I love you Lord, and I lift my voice . . .* The debate in my mind began, though it was a brief one. I wanted to battle, but I knew surrender would come. I still had questions.

The hurt still scorched, but carrying the grief day in and day out created a longing for rest that I knew could be found in only one place. I'd been asked before if I was mad at God, and really it's a fairly common response during the stages of mourning. However, I could honestly say my anger was tempered by my need for Him. I was so mixed up and lost that I knew He was the only one who could truly handle me in this state and somehow mend the wounds I thought might never heal. My desperation outweighed my sense of injustice, but love after pain—after dreams have been shattered—that was going to be a process. That Sunday morning, I was processing even as the Lord was drawing me unto Himself with a new addition to the song.

The bridge, which I had not recognized began slowly, "How I love You . . . How I love You . . . How I love You . . . Jesus." Again, with intensity, "How I love You . . . How I love You . . . How I love You . . . Jesus." The cadence was rhythmic and melodic, beckoning my heart from its cage. Voices erupted throughout the congregation singing the simple refrain with passion, louder and louder in my ears. My heart beat inside my head, and I gasped for air. *Lift my voice?!* I stole furtive glances at the faces around me filled with peace, but inside me a panic welled. The chorus continued, over and over. I stared at the ceiling with beseeching eyes and surrendered my voice. I opened my mouth to release the profession my spirit yearned to sing. A hoarse and faint "How . . ." was all I could muster at first as I swallowed the rest of the words in a choked sob. These words meant something. This wasn't rote, mindless repetition, and it was unbelievably hard.

And again, the bridge played. Wasn't anybody tired of this song yet? It was as if the worship leader was on assignment from God to lead this song over and over until I sang each and every word through. When I opened my mouth again, I could barely hear my own raspy refrain, but I heard the sweetest voice say, "I hear your whisper." Tears streamed down my face, as they often did, but love, oh deepest love, flooded my soul. He heard me. He knew where I was in space and heart, and the sacrifice of praise was beautiful to Him, albeit throaty, snotty, and bleary-eyed. He did not require a songbird; a whisper was enough. I didn't have to be whole, and He wasn't daunted by my questions or hesitation. He heard my whisper. I don't doubt that the God of the universe is capable of hearing all things as He is moving mountains and parting seas, but the fact that He took the time to tell me He'd heard ME, speaks of His heart and patience.

It was months before we sang that song again, despite its apparent popularity that first day. In fact, it was so long that it didn't initially bring back any memory of "whisper Sunday." It wasn't until the third or fourth round of "How I love You" that I became very aware of the bold clarity of my voice, singing through smiles without a care. I inhaled suddenly—not in hesitation but rather a gasp of enlightened freedom. He'd brought me through. My whisper sowed the seeds of worship to come—free, joyous, and unashamed.

10

The irony was not lost on me that we were taking Dustin to Paradise, although town folklore stated the name had a less scrupulous origin. The story goes that during the gold rush, the Pair o' Dice Saloon was a favorite destination for many weary from panning for riches. Though the saloon's existence has not been substantiated, there is a historic railroad map with "Paradice" labeled by the town dot. Others argue the legend is complete rubbish, but it's the story Dustin told me, so it's the one I choose to believe. Naturally, he preferred it best. The town is hidden in northern California with a population of roughly 25,000 residents, gatekeepers to the Sierra Nevada Mountains. Regardless of which origin story is true, the scenery boasts heavenly craftsmanship. Though Paradise was the end goal, the trip to California began to take on a life of its own, becoming both a personal pilgrimage and a time of healing for my family.

I decided I would fly out to Chico first and spend a few

days by myself to work through the previous five months and prepare for the road ahead. I spared no expense and found a darling bed and breakfast on the outskirts of the city surrounded by orchards. Meanwhile, my parents and brother would spend those days driving to meet me in time for Seth and me to embark on our journey. My mom suggested that we take our time returning to Texas by way of a road trip through northern California for some family time. We always had the best times on road trips, and I realized my family was grieving too. The time together would be good for us, and the change of scenery, particularly such gorgeous scenery, would be therapeutic.

For me, it was not just about taking Dustin to his earthly resting place; it was about escaping the familiar so I could just be and think and walk and journal and cry or not cry. It would be a shame to travel all that way and never see the sites he'd spoken of so fondly, and maybe, just maybe, I'd find him there. I remember whispering into the darkness of my bedroom one night in a moment of vulnerability, "Will you meet me there?"

Getting to Chico was a quick flight into Sacramento followed by an uneventful drive past many a fresh fruit stand. I had no trouble finding the inn, but as I drove through Chico, it was hard to focus on the roads as I took in the sites to see which ones registered from his stories. The inn was tucked behind rod iron gates and was a modest ranch-style home showcasing a magazine-worthy front yard. The backyard rivaled the front as perfectly manicured gardens and topiaries flanked either side of the swimming pool. The inn had also become a favorite wedding destination, and I could easily see why. Inside the home felt more like an art gallery with each room featuring a different artist. All the paintings in my room were of local orchards, which I particularly loved. It was the smallest of the rooms, but I knew when I saw it that it was special.

Not long after my arrival, Tori, the owner, brought me a tray of waters, ice, fruit, nuts, and blood orange Italian soda. She was about my height, probably in her late fifties, and her short curls bounced in a naturally gray bob. She wore a black chef's jacket and had the sun-soaked tan of a true Californian. Her hands were weathered, yet soft, having seen years in the garden and on the cooking line. She bustled around me but not in a manner that was unsettling—more like a fairy godmother seeking to wave away my worries and cares.

After making sure I was settled in my room with my refreshments, she said she was going out to water the plants, but I was to call her if I needed anything. She said she would be "Mom Tori" for my stay. She knew the purpose of my visit, and though I'd run away from home, she figured one always needs a mom. I felt I could trust her with Dustin and even showed her a picture of him. She commented on his smile and said he was still smiling. That made my heart smile, and I hung on every word of encouragement she uttered after. I went into town for dinner and to get my bearings. I came back to a turned-down bed with the promise of coffee by my door in the morning to enjoy while I got ready for breakfast. It was just too much, and I loved every bit!

True to her word, there was a tray of coffee by the door the next day with a note—"Today is big with blessings! You are blessed." I took the tray to my leather arm chair, curled up, and clutched the note with a smile. It would be my first day to venture out, but I was in no hurry. I felt I had much on my heart to journal over breakfast. Today was the day I'd finally go to the farmer's market, and I had a special summer dress picked out for the occasion.

I came to the dining room to find a place setting for one. I was apparently the only guest that morning, and as such was stunned by the plate before me. I was served art in the form of a melon bowl overflowing with the freshest strawberries, blueberries, peaches, raspberries, and basil with a dollop of heaven on top, and "JOY" stared back at me on the plate spelled out in cinnamon. The fruit medley was followed by a whole grain bagel, poached eggs with bacon, homegrown tomatoes, and cottage cheese.

It was good I was by myself because it was a marathon breakfast—partially due to the feast before me, but more so because I would journal a page or two between mouthfuls and then gaze out the window while the birds sang to me. It was surreal, and I was completely content in the quiet with my thoughts and Tori's occasional welcomed interruption. She said I was not to rush but just enjoy. On other mornings, she would pull up a chair and let me tell Dustin stories, and she was kind enough to listen intently till I was finished.

Later that day, I returned to the inn for some poolside reading. I'd been reading *The Year of Magical Thinking* by Joan Didion, sent to me by my aunt. It is a fascinating masterpiece detailing the year after she lost her husband, screenwriter John Gregory Dunne. Her prose is heavy but comforting, like the oversized, protective lead bib they drape over your body at the dentist's office before X-rays. I'm always strangely relaxed under its weight as if I feel instantly warm and contained, though slightly suffocated. Didion's husband died suddenly as well, and I drank in her words of shock, sadness, and confusion. Each page more melancholy than the first, but I liked it that way.

Didion's honest suffering gave me license to feel openly and not be too quick to process emotions, as if one deals with grief in assembly-line fashion. I was actually quite sick of the word "process." Cheese is processed, not feelings, not love—both great and perplexing. The word is mechanical and orderly, and none of this was, though I'd tried to make it so.

Yet in Chico, at this lovely inn, the machines seemed to grind to a halt, and I indulged Didion's magical thinking. The next day, I went for an early morning run. I pounded the pavement for a while till I was overcome by the temptation of the orchards and veered into their dark rows. I was hidden from the road and bounced carefree on the trampoline of soft earth beneath me. *Well, as carefree as this rule follower could be despite blatantly trespassing on someone's property and trampling through their livelihood.* It was liberating, and at one point, I followed a beam of sunlight to a small clearing where I sat and had Sunday service. I prayed, and then I just listened because He had things to speak to me.

The run had been a good decision on many levels, and it

bolstered my appetite for the delicious spread awaiting me back at Tori's. My cinnamon-sprinkled word of the day was "LIFE." All days really should begin with a dusting of inspiration on your plate.

The time in Chico was a gift, and as a wife, I felt like it was the trip he would've planned. I secretly wondered if there had been some scheming up in heaven surrounding those three perfect days, and if he was enjoying every special detail that fell into place with pride. I had this precious capsule of memories from my time there that I would savor forever, but to try stay longer might undo the magic. Midnight approached. It was time to leave Narnia, and I might never be back.

My family met me at the inn that morning, Dustin in tow. It was time. I was ready, and yet I was hesitant to leave this magical place where he felt alive and so close. My dad had already plotted out our drive to Paradise, but from there, our hopes rested on a printed email with vague instructions from a complete stranger. My quest for this mysterious place led to many dead ends. All the names I thought he called this place did not seem to register on Google as an actual destination. Discouraged but undaunted, I kept looking until we finally had a break when my dad sent me a random picture he found on the Internet.

Dustin had once showed him a picture of the "emerald pond" as we began to refer to it, and this picture looked just like it. For the life of me, I couldn't remember, but I began to pursue this lead. It was all we had. One search led me to a youth leader in California who'd posted the same picture on his youth group's blog from a previous visit. I hesitated reaching out to him, but having no other options, I sent him a long email, shamelessly playing every card I could think of so he would a) know I was sincere and b) not let me down! The kindness of strangers might as well be a subtitle for this chapter. He, like so many others along the way, became a precious soul to me, a guide sent from heaven, albeit with cryptic instructions.

Once we parked at the base of the mountain, the directions shifted from roads to landmarks, and by landmarks, I mean curves in the path, direction of the creek—basically nothing of significance. Seth and I left our parents to pray by the car while we ascended the steep incline of loose sand gravel, hiking straight towards the sun. I became tired from the thinness of the air, the heat, and our aimless wandering. We walked uphill for what seemed like a mile or two only to find that we were miserably off track. We retraced our steps, and for a moment I began to panic. *What if we're lost? What if we never find it? We've come all this way, and what if we wander in circles? I made a promise!* But as quickly as the panic flared up, it was replaced with a calming peace. I thought for a moment about the countless friends and family who were covering this journey in prayer, and I knew there was no way we couldn't find our path with support of that caliber. We would not fail.

Sure enough, we found it, though not without great effort. The hike was a bit more challenging than anticipated, or maybe I was just more out of shape than I thought. We had to climb up steep hills and over slippery boulders of granite. I lost my footing, scraped knees, and became incredibly grateful for my brother's patience and uncharacteristic gentleness as we navigated the unfamiliar to ultimately discover Paradise.

It was breathtaking, truly just like Dustin had always said, and so *alive* with beauty, a testament to the Great Artist. In retrospect, it was right for the road to be so challenging, a sacrificial labor of love for someone loved so much by so many. Tucked away in all the rocks and trees was a resting place befitting for such a unique and tender-hearted man.

We stood in amazement and wonder, both from the beauty of the site and the completion of the journey. The water did have an emerald hue and was completely clear. The deep pond was surrounded by giant boulders and framed with trees. A small waterfall fed the pool gently with calming streams. While I was taking it all in, my brother was already ripping off his shirt preparing for a dive.

"What are you doing?!" I asked.

"I wanna dive in," he said with a "why not" kind of shrug.

"Yeah, Dustin said they used to jump here and swim," I said. "Well, if you're jumping I should jump. I mean we came all this way, right?"

"Well then jump," he yelled from the top.

"Um, you jump first; I just need to sit for a while."

My nerves were getting the best of me, but another part of me was irked by his playfulness. *Did he forget why we're here? This is not supposed to be fun*. Then again, what was it supposed to be?

How better to honor Dustin than with a little mischievousness? I knew if left alone I could sit and brood for hours, and in that moment, I wanted to be left alone. Instead I was splashed with cold water as Seth took a leap off the rocks emerging with a "Woohoo!" Now the height of the jump was not the only deterrent but the cold water awaiting. I stalled longer. I'm not quite sure what I expected, but I felt antsy. I looked across the pond to the bushes that lined the other shore. I stared hard between the branches, willing him to emerge from them and give me a wave or a smile, something to say I'd arrived. This was the place, and he was proud.

Dustin did not appear. Instead, another hiking couple interrupted our solitude with flirtatious laughter and bare bodies. I was initially quite irritated by their presence and then appalled at their casual swim through my sacred waters. Oh, this was not part of the plan. My brother awkwardly waited for me to make a move. I finally decided I might as well jump. I'd later regret it if I didn't, and maybe the waves would scare away our intruders.

I was glad I did. My body cut through the water, and I felt enveloped by the depths only to rise refreshed. The lovebirds did not leave though. In fact, I was almost completely dry from sitting out/stalling when Seth reminded me of the time and that our poor parents had likely been waiting for hours. He wasn't trying to rush me, but we had no way of knowing how long it would be before we had the place to ourselves. It was going to have to happen despite their presence, with little ceremony or fuss. Though I knew that would've been Dustin's preference, I felt like I was cheating the moment. My heart began to race. *I can't do this. This isn't right. It's not supposed to go this way. You were supposed to meet me here!*

Seconds later, a stunning red and orange butterfly flew seemingly from the bushes towards me and circled my head, granting peace. Butterflies to me were a special reminder of him because we'd enjoyed them at an outdoor sanctuary on our honeymoon. It was a beautiful reminder that I could do this, a gracious gift from God.

It was time, and though I was emotionally ready, I couldn't bear the thought of having an audience, so I told my brother we had to find a secluded spot. I could almost hear Dustin rolling with laughter from heaven as we suspiciously snuck around the rocks to a shaded corner, casting furtive glances back at the couple. Seth was certain they assumed we were carrying drugs in the backpack or had other nefarious intentions. I couldn't help but nervously giggle. *Great, now I'm laughing. This is so wrong.* The moment demanded at least a modicum of reverence, so I whispered a sincere prayer, and we did what we'd set out to do back in March. I didn't quite know what to make of the anticlimactic final moment, but I now understand the journey was as much the purpose as the destination. And there was one more demonstration of grace to conclude the goodbye.

I bought flowers two days before at the Chico Farmer's Market, a large mixed bouquet for my host and a small bundle of fragrant tuberose for my room during the stay. As I packed up my room, I lamented the fact that I'd found nothing the previous day to leave behind after scattering his ashes. My eyes scanned the room at a loss and then paused on the simple white sprigs of tuberose. Ah, it was perfect, flowers for his grave, and I secured my portable bouquet safely in the backpack. The Lord cared about even the little things, and at the pond's edge I was able to set them adrift into the emerald waters. It was such a sweet pleasure to have them with me, a lovely souvenir from the farmer's market he enjoyed and a simple, but perfect gift to leave behind. It was well with my soul.

The finality of spreading the ashes of my husband was still very jarring, no matter the preparation, but I was grateful to be able to honor his life with "something truly majestic" as Jack Nicholson's character did for his friend played by Morgan Freeman in *The Bucket List.* We watched the movie a week before he died. In thinking about it now, I can't help but smile at the last line when the narrator said that Edward, Jack Nicholson's character, would have loved this because he was "buried on the mountain, and that was against the law."[2] As we hiked back down towards the car, the path took us along a rock wall with carvings, *ok etched graffiti*, left by previous visitors. It was all tastefully done, and as I stared at the messages and names, I was inspired to further step outside my box. I grabbed a shard of rock on the ground and began to carve "Dustin." In the end, he did have a stone marker; though I'm certain this was much more his style, and, like Edward, Dustin would've been proud of his baby breaking a few rules in the process.

11

In the final months leading up to the California trip, I became anxious, though not for the reasons you would expect. Yes, the intent of the journey was ever on my mind; however, the act of spreading his ashes was less unsettling than the constant reminder of his absence. Other than our honeymoon, we had not traveled together, and if ever there was a trip we would've loved to plan, it would've been this one. I both anticipated and feared Chico in particular. What if I was completely miserable there? What if it was endless salt on deep wounds? Even the road trip after with my family made me nervous. I couldn't stand the thought of not sharing these experiences with him, so I decided I would just have to find a way.

Weeks before my departure, I devised a plan with a friend from Dallas over dinner. I was going to send postcards to Dustin as I traveled, and since I only knew one way to heaven that wasn't marked by a P.O. Box, I would mail them back to myself in Texas. She agreed it was perfect. Days before I left, a letter arrived with a book of stamps and a sweet note from my friend. She wanted to make sure I'd have plenty of postage for my precious correspondence. Her gift touched my heart deeply.

The postcards provided an outlet for the pressure and an escape I often retreated to on our trip. I chose not to advertise my coping strategy, but one morning over breakfast, my brother called me out. He and I were on the patio of the hotel, and I was intently filling every square inch of a postcard with my musings.

"Who do you keep writing postcards to?" he said with a twinge of annoyance.

"Well . . . I'm writing them to Dustin," I said and then paused expecting a look of *well now she's lost it.*

Instead, he stared at me for a quiet minute and casually said, "I get that." He then told me about a college basketball coach who wrote letters to his wife after she died. *Ah, then yes, he did get it; and somehow all things go back to sports.* We smiled at each other, and he went back to eating as I returned to writing.

Days after I arrived back home, the cards started trickling in, and I put them away in a box to open on a special day. Where I couldn't find postcards, I found cards with images of something memorable of the destination. In today's age of cellphones and the ability to text pictures instantaneously, postcards may seem archaic, but they were little 3x5 blessings of sanity to me.

Chico

My Great Love,

Well, I did it. I went to your beloved Chico Farmer's Market, and yes, you were right—ten times over. I couldn't believe all the fresh flowers. It was amazing! I would come and buy flowers all the time. There was one particular flower, the licianthus, that I was particularly drawn to. I may to try to plant it (yes, I said plant) because it does well in heat. We'll see about Texas heat. I felt so loved and embraced by the community. I've been able to share our story to a few vendors, and they've responded with such heart-felt emotion and sincerity. It's like you must have sent a memo to the community telling them I was coming and to take special care of me—because they have. The photographer who I bought this card from gave me a free magnet just to show she cared. I chose the one that matched this card . . . I've been looking for souvenirs of us. I found this lovely necklace with glass the color of your eyes. It's very dainty and perfect, my secret pleasure to carry you with me . . .

Mendocino

Dear Dustin,

It is everything Mom said and more. It's the most lovely seaside town I've ever seen, the perfect setting for a novel. They had the coolest little grocery store ever, like a mini, quaint Whole Foods. You would've loved it. There are flowers everywhere! These trumpet flowers were longer than my face! Although I'm sure the flowers you see far exceed this. Seth says once you've seen one garden, you've seen them all. Unfortunately, Mom did not take my advice, and we were stuck without a car while Seth and Papa golfed. And all the shops had closed. For two hours, we wandered.

Fort Bragg

Dear Dustin,

This portion of the trip with my family has been good, but I get tired. It takes real effort not to think of you, though I think of us every second and how we would've had such a blast. In Fort Bragg, we ate at a restaurant called Egg Head which was like something off of Tripled D. It was so crammed with only six tables. We had amazing omelets. The next day we ate at a pizza place with a very rude guy. Somehow we ended up at a fish and chips place that looked more like a Chinese restaurant inside. False advertising! Lots of laughs. I keep picturing your funny expressions.

Yosemite National Park

Dear Dustin,

On our way up to Yosemite, we went to Putah Creek Grill in Winters. I saw it on Triple D a few weeks ago. It was neat, but of course I ordered the wrong thing instead of playing it safe. Everyone teased me about it last night. I'm sure you would've joined right in. Yosemite was beautiful; it's like a city hidden in the trees. Your brother texted me while we were there and mentioned how much you loved it. I can imagine! Taking you with me . . .

In the second drawer of my nightstand, I secured the stacks of postcards, greeting cards, and letters delivered to my door addressed to him. I smiled when they arrived in the mail but didn't dare open them, not just yet. On his birthday, I would finally indulge. My sister-in-law and I had already decided his birthday was a day to celebrate, so we planned a brunch date at his favorite café. It was a good plan, but I anticipated I'd need time on my own to prepare and set my alarm for an early rise.

It wasn't necessary. I woke on my own, light streaming through the blinds, and stared ahead with glazed eyes. It would've been his thirtieth birthday, and I needed to feel close to him. I decidedly threw back the covers, washed the somber off my face, and knelt before the nightstand. It was like opening a treasure chest, and I hugged the bundle of correspondence, thankful for the gift it would be to me that day. I sipped coffee on the porch and opened each letter, read every postcard, and smiled.

Reliving the trip to California and all the stops took me back to that magical place where his smile and laughter was a constant, though distant, companion. I allowed myself a few more Dear Dustins in the months to come when jotting thoughts in a journal wouldn't suffice.

12

The pain felt after the loss of someone so dear cannot be confined to a span of time or framed in a calendar year; it is fluid and sporadic. That said, there is a distinct anguish that taunts the first year following death. I call it the Year of Firsts because though each day carries a shadow of sadness, there are those milestone holidays, birthdays, and anniversaries where that person's absence is echoed by the historic or sentimental significance of the day. These "firsts" are precipitated by great dread and finally felt with the intensity of a gut punch. There's no getting around it. It will be a long, hard year, and you must close your eyes, clinch your teeth, and rip off the Band-Aid time and time again.

The holidays typically come to mind when considering the Year of Firsts because they encompass so much emotion tied to tradition and togetherness. Each one brings unique challenges depending on the memories made. Valentine's Day, though never a personal favorite, is still a celebration of love and companionship, salt on a solitary wound. Thanksgiving prompts expressions of gratitude from guests at a table with a now-empty seat. New Year's—well, you already know how I feel about New Year's. Last, but certainly not least, is Christmas, my most favorite holiday and Dustin's least. Dustin was the subtle Scrooge to my Mrs. Claus, but like a champ, he hung on for dear life through the holiday hoopla and kindly humored my elfish ways.

Christmas gloriously refuses to be confined to one day. Rather, it is an entire season of month-long cheer . . . for some. There is no reprieve following Thanksgiving; it merely serves as the kick-off to weeks of tinsel, carols, cocoa, and endless Hallmark movies, which equals endless opportunities for angst. Right on schedule, the Christmas blues hit hard and heavy that first week of December 2011.

Our office admin was practically floating on air. Finally, after six months of international separation, he would get to see his girlfriend again, and this reunion would be accompanied by a ring. He bought the ring months before, and we all teased mercilessly that he wouldn't be able to wait till January to propose. I didn't initially shy away from the pre-proposal discussions. I was genuinely excited for him, though it reminded me of another eager fellow who couldn't wait till the New Year to pop the question. As the reunion/proposal day approached, our engagement weighed on my mind.

It was the first Friday of December, the same weekend Dustin orchestrated a proposal that took me quite by surprise.

At Christmas, the picturesque village of Salado hosts the Salado Stroll where the little shops on Main Street embody seasonal charm and are decorated with endless lights and wreaths. There are carolers, Santa, carriage rides, and the mouthwatering aroma of fresh kettle corn and hot chocolate. I'd always thought it was such a romantic setting and had been hinting about the stroll to him since October. Because I was truly an unsuspecting bride, I almost sabotaged his entire plan unknowingly, but by the end of the evening we were happily engaged with much laughter to follow. Sometimes you just go with the flow, shut your mouth, and let your man sweep you off your feet. He did just that. Afterwards, we went back to our friends' house to share the news. Dustin knew that I wouldn't want a public proposal but made sure friends were available afterwards.

Watching our admin fidget and fantasize over the perfect proposal gave me a glimpse of what that day must have been like for Dustin. I smiled at the thought of that, but nothing else—and I tired of his enthusiasm. The site of him bustling down the hall began to grate on my nerves. I didn't want to hear his plans or hear of Christmas outings in general. At one point, I forcefully shut my office door and typed emails mindlessly as tears trickled down my face, but mostly I just sat and stared at the computer in disbelief. How ironic that their proposal would be so untimely planned. *Couldn't he propose another weekend, another month . . . another year?!* I so wanted to step into their blissful shoes and relive the euphoria of new love—the butterflies, the meaningful glances, and proclamations rich with sentiment and promise. I longed for the innocence and naiveté of our first December together even as I tried to avoid potentially painful landmarks in a town rich with memories.

I had just purchased my home in Salado, but this resident determined to avoid the Stroll at all costs, despite the fact that it was the town's claim to fame. One evening though, I found my resolve beginning to thaw as I drove unavoidably down Main Street on a weeknight and fell under the spell of the twinkling lights. I began to wonder if my avoidance of special places did more harm than good.

I gradually found myself talking about Dustin more frequently in the weeks to come, and in one particular shop, I told the storekeeper how we'd stopped in her store that night and how he cleverly filed away my verbal admiration for the ballerina paintings on the wall. He later surprised me with both paintings along with a host of other gifts on Christmas that year — ten to my one for him. *Does it count that I was saving for a wedding?* I don't know that she really cared as she listened with feigned interest, but it felt good to tell the story, as if I was bringing that night back to life. I realized I had to choose whether I would let those memories depress me because Dustin was gone or embrace them because they were our story—sad chapters and all.

The fact that we got engaged during the Christmas holiday did further complicate an already-difficult season. All the memories began to run together as the 25th approached with thoughts of our first Christmas as husband and wife, which included a kitschy card with the cats dressed up in Christmas plaid. That year was spent in South Texas with my relatives, a very special year of family and the exchange of traditions.

I did allow myself one Christmas concession in lieu of its being the first. I chose not to decorate—not a tree, not a wreath, not a single ornament! I had not the energy, and the decision, once made, was freeing. I did not despise everyone else's décor; I simply took a break from my own. I could celebrate the holiday in small doses at other homes, and when I was done, I needed only return to my festivity-free zone to regroup and remember at my leisure. I felt empowered by my acknowledgement of where I was emotionally, but come December 26th I was ready to hit the after-Christmas sales in search of decorations to adorn the new house next year. The Christmas spirit had not left me entirely; it just took a one-year sabbatical.

A few months after Christmas, I would stagger across the first-year finish line but not without passing our wedding anniversary, followed closely by the anniversary of his death, a loathsome day. I often felt like I swam in a fishbowl on these days because, though many would forget my grief on a regular Tuesday, holidays and anniversaries reminded them of my daily reality. It was both a blessing and a curse. I would not perform for the spectators, but just the same, I welcomed their well-wishes and prayers while I retreated to process privately. I'd walked through so many other firsts that never hit their radar—baby showers, weddings, fall/spring, trips to Whole Foods (our favorite "theme park")—that I would make it through these. With each one, messages of hope mingled in with the sadness, and I had a constant sense of heavenly companionship through this journey. The Year of Firsts brought to life the scripture, 2 Corinthians 12:9: *My grace is sufficient for you . . .*

Yes, even in this I found it to be true.

13

Labor Day weekend for most is a welcomed three-day weekend, but seeing as how Dustin's birthday typically fell into this holiday, the tone is a bit more pensive for the Stephens family. I remember the first birthday without him. As with most milestones, the anticipation was far worse than the actual day. The bittersweet celebration in his honor would commence with a party for two at Megg's, our favorite local eatery. My sister-in-law and I met for coffee, breakfast, and finally a cupcake to climax hours of Dustin stories. It was a perfect day for what it was, and he felt very near.

The second year was not quite as pleasantly planned. There was no ceremonial coffee and journal time of reflection. No remembrance lunch with April. Instead I shuffled among strangers through airports and sat crammed between a select two of them on a plane for umpteen hours. I was returning from my cousin's wedding in Connecticut carrying on one weekend bag and a bladder infection. Needless to say, I was distracted from the reverence of the day, and though sweet, reassuring texts were sent from friends who remembered, I was largely emotionless.

The following weekend, my church was having a potluck after service, and I knew exactly what I would bring—Four Layer Heaven. It's a relatively simple dessert of, you guessed it, four yummy layers: shortbread, cream cheese and sugar, chocolate, Cool Whip, and a few other things. I'd had it many times growing up, but it became special when I found out it was Dustin's favorite dessert and what he requested for his birthday each year in lieu of cake.

The first time I made Four Layer Heaven for Dustin we weren't even dating, though our friends said we were. Typical of the lost in love, they're the last to know . . . or better yet, admit. It wasn't technically on his birthday but shortly thereafter at our friend's house. I had lovingly made each layer knowing he had not had his favorite treat this year. My homemade surprise was a well-timed rescue because earlier that day, he professed his love for me, and the slow mover I am wasn't ready with a response . . . not just yet. The drive to the house that evening was a bit awkward, as you can imagine. Though I had not verbalized the words yet, I felt them with every fiber of my being, and it was only a matter of time before I said them.

The Four Layer Heaven sat in my lap tightly sealed, the lid hiding its goodness. I suppose somewhere inside I knew the mantle had passed to me, and I would now be carrying on the tradition for birthdays to come. Looking back, I relish the picture of that care free couple, full of anticipation for a life of adventure with the other. I can still see his face as he rounded the kitchen wall with a surprised smile and a plate piled high with his birthday dessert.

"Did you do this for me?!" he said as I nodded, beaming with pride and basking in his happiness.

He then announced to everyone in the room what a special gesture this was in light of his birthday a few weeks earlier, his aversion to cake, etc. I did not say, "I love you" that day, but it showed. Fortified with that knowledge, he was patient to wait for my reciprocation. (It came only four days later.)

The memory of his youthful pleasure and smile that day made me resolve to make his dessert at the start of every September. In years to come, no one may understand the significance, but I will. Birthdays are always to be celebrated. It was when Dustin's life began, and so it will always be cherished for him and him alone. On this Sunday after his birthday, with years of healing behind me, I was rested and recuperated—a much better state for baking. I whipped up all the ingredients, slobbered over the spoon, whisk, and bowl, and put the finished product in the fridge with little sentiment or drama. I was fine. It was a sweet thing to do, and I would enjoy a slice with his memory the next day.

I awoke that Sunday in plenty of time to have leisurely coffee and get ready, only to later scramble at the last minute—a fairly common event. I grabbed the dress that stood out as the most ready to go and quickly fumbled with my makeup. The dress was navy with taupe polka dots and a flirty skirt. I always feel a tad vintage in it, especially when I wear bright red lipstick, which I did to detract from my wet bun. There was no hidden agenda in the choice, just the quick fix to my tardiness. Yet as I stood facing the mirror, ready to head out the door, something gnawed at me. In a flash, I was in my dress standing at the back of the church three years prior, late as well. I was stalling to determine the least distractive entrance into the sanctuary and bumped into Dustin. It had to have been only our second or third conversation, but he made the most of his window and initiated a humorous string of comedic retorts that were intended to make me laugh, but fell a bit flat. Now THAT made me laugh.

He loved to tell the story of our conversation that day because he knew it wasn't his best work. It was very schoolboy-meets-pigtails-and-ribbons, and today the memory yanked my heart to a stop. The Four Layer Heaven and I drove in silence as a string of those very early memories played like a movie reel. There was such innocence to his admiration then and an adoration that eventually (and by eventually I mean in very little time at all) melted my heart.

I was so grateful to find an empty pew where I could stand in the dimly lit crowd of worshippers and feel somewhat hidden in my grief. I gripped my hands tightly as the memories continued to flow in concert with my tears. Tears I hadn't cried in a while—hot tears that melted off my chin.

I think of Dustin every day, but it had been some time since I'd grieved him so intensely, since I'd missed him with that burning ache. I stood paralyzed by the random wave of emotions triggered on a typical Sunday morning by an unsuspecting navy, polka-dot dress. After the service, I was torn. I wanted to escape to our park downtown and allow myself to weep openly, but there was the luncheon and the Four Layer Heaven. I was tempted to just ask someone to return the pan to me later, but after visiting with a few people and putting on a strong face, I felt my emotional instability settle. *You've got this!* And I did until I reached the end of the line with the desserts.

I pointed quietly at mine to request a piece, and the children's pastor vigorously stabbed the fluffy layers with a pie server and scooped out my portion. In that moment, the pie server may as well have been thrust into my heart. Even I was surprised at my intense reaction, but my eyes immediately started to fill. *This is Dustin's cake! How dare you treat it with such disregard?* Thank goodness I never vocalized the crazy thoughts whirling in my head. I had enough sense to remove myself to a corner of the room where I could focus on eating and keeping my mouth shut.

In retrospect, I'm sure it was the culmination of many things. His birthday being felt on a subconscious level, the making of his favorite dessert, the change of the weather . . . it's strange how the significant and the slight come together to form the perfect storm of emotions. I did drive to the park after lunch and walked along the path for some time. I'm grateful I have that park. It's always there for me when I need to be in a place where he was, where we were. By the end of the day, I was calm and at peace. I had mourned and remembered, and when you lose someone you've loved so deeply, it is right that you should have these days. In some ways, the catharsis is good, dare I say refreshing. It is a reminder of the passion and the depth of the life with that person, a reminder that you haven't forgotten even the little things you're so fearful you will and a cleansing of the pain you stifle on a day-to-day basis in order to survive.

14

The Gospels recount many of Jesus' miracles while on earth, and three of the four chronicle the story of Jairus, a ruler in the synagogue who petitioned Jesus for the life of his dying daughter. Scripture tells of the desperate attempt of a father to draw Jesus away from the crowd so they could make haste to Jairus' home where Jesus could heal his daughter. Along the way, the story abruptly shifts from Jairus' plight to that of a tormented woman slowly bleeding to death as a result of a lifelong condition. Her plague prompts a demonstration of great faith, which causes Jesus to pause and address her need. The exchange, though not lengthy, delays Jesus just long enough for messengers to arrive pronouncing the death of Jairus' daughter. Our pastor chose to preach from this passage in the fifth chapter of Mark one Sunday. The sermon was pivotal for me.

I was raised in church and had heard the story of Jairus and the woman with the blood condition countless times. I was tempted to half tune out until the pastor took a different approach to his retelling of the story. He taught solely from the perspective of Jairus and invited us into the frantic mind of a father who submitted an enormous request to Jesus with a limited window of time.

Mark 5: 22-23: *And when he saw him, he fell at his feet and begged him earnestly, "My little daughter lies at the point of death. Come and lay your hands on her that she may be healed, and she will live." So Jesus went with him.*

Great. All seems well, until Jairus must stand back in horror as Jesus deviates from the path to minister to another woman in need of dire healing. It's completely understandable to the reader. What was Jesus supposed to do? Ignore the woman? If you're Jairus, the answer is a resounding "Yes!" He had everything to lose. He'd defied decorum and status to kneel before this Nazarene and beg for his daughter's life. If you're Jairus, you're mad at Jesus for stopping; time was of the essence. You view Jesus' compassion towards one woman as an act of abandonment to your family. How are you then supposed to respond when you see your friends approaching with somber faces, and you realize it has been all for naught? Because Jesus stopped to tend to the woman, your daughter is dead.

I suppose I'd never given the delay much thought in the past because I knew the end of the story. What did it matter to dwell on that when ultimately, Jesus raised the daughter to life, and the family was restored? Perspective. It changes everything when you approach the familiar with fresh eyes. In my pastor's version, the supporting character became the lead, and his viewpoint registered with me. I was also hearing the story for the first time since my own walk of desperation and the messengers of death that followed.

My life with Dustin was a gift from the get-go, an unlikely love story with great promise and purpose. We complemented each other well and differed enough to keep things interesting and balanced. When my husband left for Tyler to visit his friend, I had no inkling of his impending death, yet I struggled with his absence just the same. We were desperately seeking clarity at that time having been dealt some challenging blows early on in our marriage. I distinctly remember cleaning out the bathroom cabinets while he was away and listening to a podcast of the pastor from my hometown. His words poured from the speakers into my heart, and I stopped what I was doing to bury my head in my hands and pray, not out of dread but with an expectation of good things to come. The next day I received the call.

I could identify with the Jairus portrayed from the pulpit that morning. I too had called upon the Lord. I was certain He was on His way to my home, but it appeared someone else's need was more pressing. The message was like a hot poker thrust into my heart, kindling embers of emotions I'd ignored. The rage and pain spilled over my cheeks, and though I'd become deft at the silent cry, I had to choke down small sobs that threatened to give me away.

As is customary at the end of our church services, the pastor invites those with a need to come to the front of the church and pray with a staff member while the congregation disperses. Within seconds, I stood before my pastor and his wife, racking with sobs.

"I . . . I . . . I am Jairus!" I said through snot and tears.

I think I even motioned to myself to emphasize the point I was so ineptly communicating. It was a weird prayer request, really more of a loaded statement, but for once, I cared nothing for what anyone around me thought. A volcano of emotions from a deeply hidden place of pain spewed all over the altar, and I let the lava flow. As much as it hurt, this wound had festered long enough, and He brought to the surface what I would've kept buried. I was thankful to be with my "safe people" in that moment; they'd love me regardless of the spectacle. It was because they loved me so much that they cried with me, and another layer of healing began.

God could handle my anger. He'd been waiting for me to surrender it to Him so it could stop suffocating me. Not a stitch of makeup remained after that tear fest, but I left the sanctuary with my head held high and my heart light. There are some things in this life we will not understand nor be given an adequate explanation. It seemed my story did not have the triumphant ending of Jairus'; I know many who would say the same of their own story. But perhaps triumphs and victories must also be viewed through the lens of perspective. I would have to trust Him in that. I'd been angry, borderline bitter, with God, yet I knew I could not navigate this road without Him. No one else could fully know or understand the crazy in my head and my heart, and I could either fight His companionship or welcome it. I chose the latter.

Learning to Ride Again

15

I've heard it said that memories are like souvenirs of time. Often we don't know the moments of life that we'll one day wish we'd savored more or obsessed over less. It's like going on vacation and opting not to purchase that special memento only to wish you had once back at home where the item can't be found.

Of course there is no going back in time, and you cannot purchase souvenirs from the past—that is, unless you know the loop hole. I discovered that though time travel was not an option, I could purchase items that reminded me of a memory, and it had the same effect. I called them "souvenirs of us," and I stumbled upon them regularly that first year. Maybe I willed them to be as I searched for meaning and a connection to our lives before. It was true retail therapy, and I gave little pause to consider the monetary cost. In those moments, the peace and nearness of him was priceless.

More often than not, my souvenirs did not require a splurge.

Their subjective value, though conceded by others, was truly only felt by me. One day it was a set of butterfly coffee mugs; another day it was a sentimental frame. And then came the day when serendipity turned a couple of discarded buttons into a portal to the past.

There's a small, eclectic boutique I love to shop at in Temple. I visited more frequently when we had our apartment just a block away, but it's still worth an out-of-the-way stop every once in a while. I love to zigzag through the displays and pick up various items for a closer look or feel the soft fabrics between my fingers. I take my time, because if you rush, you're bound to miss something, something small and perhaps of little value to the casual eye.

It sat in a little glass dish, clearly not a featured piece of jewelry but someone's craftiness on display. I glanced out of curiosity and then picked up the make-shift ring for a closer look. *Huh. An elastic band with three black buttons stacked on top like a pyramid. Cute as a button!*

It was no surprise that Dustin became a regular at my church upon moving to Texas. After all, his sister attended there, and the pastors were her in-laws. We'd long heard stories of April's brother—a rebel with a heart of gold and a magnetic personality, so naturally I introduced myself his first Sunday to make him feel welcome as a consideration for April mixed with a little bit of curiosity. I told myself I was not personally vested in his time here one way or the other, but then he kept popping up at different events and gatherings to where he was hard to avoid.

There was no denying that magnetic personality.

One particular summer Sunday, most of the congregation stayed after church for a luncheon. *We take the whole "breaking bread together" thing seriously.* As it was a typically warm day, I dressed in navy and white seersucker slacks with a fitted white, short-sleeved top, accented by a chunky red necklace and red floral ring for a pop of color. I stood across from him in line as we inched towards the buffet, and my tall, red wedges ensured I looked him square in the eyes. It was an outfit born out of seasonal necessity, not entirely meant to impress, which is why his obvious look of appreciation and candid remark took me aback.

"Well, aren't you just as cute as a button!" he said with a smile as wide as the summer in Texas is long.

"Cute as a button? What are you, eighty?" I blurted out.

The irony of it was that if anyone had a knack for nostalgia, it was me and the ninety-year-old woman I kept hidden inside. I think I badgered him about the old-fashioned expression out of shock and replied sharply without savoring the 30's era compliment I'd just received. The outburst worked to my favor. My witty retort won him over and was rewarded with booming laughter, the classic Dustin chuckle with head thrown back and dancing eyes. I was "cute as a button" and found that his admiration made him rather dapper at that.

I slipped the elastic band on my finger and stared at my button jewels. The ring had to be mine, insurance to keep the random memory with me always. My five-dollar investment proved to be quite the conversation starter. Most people had not seen a button ring, and they were fascinated by its simplicity. Depending on the person, I would entrust the story of our quirky exchange, and it was also received with smiles. One of the cheapest items in my jewelry box has now become one of the most valuable.

When one enjoys food as much as we did, there's bound to be many memories tied to tasty treats. *I practically wrote a novel in my journal after visiting Whole Foods for the first time without him.* We lived just up the road from Austin, an eclectic culinary mecca, and naturally, some of the best souvenirs of us were flavors found within its city limits. Trips to Austin are still marked by local eats and, of course, shopping.

I love to shop, clearly, but I am always looking for unique pieces that "speak to me." I can't always afford boutique prices, but I enjoy the variety they offer as opposed to racks of retail monotony at chain stores. A few years ago, my friend discovered the perfect solution to our lack of local boutique options and bank account. Le Garage was a biannual weekend bazar in Austin where boutiques and regional designers would come together to sell the previous season's clothes and jewelry at discounted rates. It sounded heavenly, and I had big plans of acquiring a new wardrobe that day, as did my friend. She was a few months pregnant with her first child and determined to somehow avoid maternity clothes for the remainder of the nine months while still maintaining her sense of style. She was on a mission.

While she quickly got lost in the frenzy of women crowding mirrors and make-shift dressing rooms, I slowly wandered the aisles. It was nice to get lost in the room of strangers, and though I saw many pretty things, I found few made me reach for my wallet. This similar phenomenon occurs regularly in IKEA. I'm overwhelmed by the endless maze of options that invariably I end up leaving with no more than a spatula because my brain can process little else. *Well, a spatula and maybe a cinnamon roll.* Le Garage was lovely, but overwhelming, so I was content to browse. Just when I thought I'd reached my capacity for walking and crowds, I discovered a booth towards the back of the hall with cutting boards and coasters featuring pictures of famous Austin landmarks. I glanced over pictures of the Capitol, the "You're My Butter Half" mural, and other recognizable photo op destinations, but it was a small square coaster with a giant pink cupcake atop an Airstream trailer that caught my eye. *Well, hey there, cupcake . . .*

It was the height of the cupcake craze, and we'd been carried right along with the hysteria. Those were the days of cupcake shops popping up on every corner while cupcake cookbooks flew off the shelves. It was also when the hit series *Cupcake Wars* was at its peak, and we sat on the edge of our seats, week after week, in anticipation of concoctions made from random mystery ingredients. Though we knew we would never be asked to serve on the official judges' panel, we voiced our criticisms and praise as if we were at least in the running. Dustin didn't cheer on sports teams, he rooted for bakers and chefs, and after a couple innings of *Iron Chef* or *Chopped*, he'd toss around a few dishes in the kitchen and recreate their plays. For someone who was not a sweets person, he quickly became enamored with cupcakes, and I gladly obliged. Inspired by the greats on TV, we'd come up with our own combos of frostings and fillings, most of which never made it past our imaginations.

One afternoon, we were enjoying lunch at our favorite café, and the waitress asked if we wanted dessert, specifically their newest cupcake addition. At that time, the café was still fairly new, and they were doing a contest to promote their bakery. Customers were asked to submit names for the Jane Doe cupcake, and there would be a prize for the winning name chosen. We were more than up for the challenge and deftly inserted our forks into the mound of frosting to extract the perfect bite of cake, filling, and topping. The meticulous analysis of flavors and textures that followed was rather ridiculous, and we poured over ideas as if we were naming our first-born child. The cream filling in the center was a pale pink, which reminded Dustin of a heart, but "heart" would simply not do. This name had to be special, so we enlisted the help of an accomplished linguist—my grandfather. He speaks many languages, including Italian, and let's be honest, pretty much anything sounds better in Italian.

Now explaining the purpose of the call to my eighty-plus-year-old grandfather only added to the hilarity of the scene. He wears hearing aids, and the topic of conversation was so random that I was forced to speak loudly and slowly to explain our request. He was only mildly amused by the quest to name a cupcake but obliged my impromptu vocabulary quiz with the stipulation that we cut him in on the winnings. Finally, after much deliberation, Dustin and I decided on a name: *Cuore Dolce.* Cuore means heart in Italian, and dolce means sweet. I assumed that, like Spanish, the adjective in Italian must come after the noun. *I don't know that it does, but it flowed better that way so that's how we wrote it down . . . being the linguists that we were.* We were very proud. Sadly, we didn't win. The Big Duper won. *Big Duper?!* It's still a sore subject.

Our cupcake fascination became a traveling companion. On many a weekend, we would plan food excursions to Austin. Austin was a short drive away from home but a lovely escape into a creative world that suited Dustin well. It was the ultimate field trip with Whole Foods, farmer's markets, restaurants, and food trucks tempting our palates. We were food truck enthusiasts, and it should come as no surprise that one of our sentimental favorites was Hey Cupcake! I don't know if it was the actual cupcakes or the giant model cupcake with pink frosting on the top of their truck that made us fans. Regardless, it was a favorite stamp in our food passport. For all of our many trips to Austin, there are no pictures of us in front of the state capitol, but by golly, we've got a slew of pictures in front of Hey Cupcake! Priorities.

My friend and I left Le Garage a little lopsided. She juggled multiple bags of clothes to accommodate her growing pregnancy belly while my three purchases fit into one small gift bag. I was perfectly content with my treasures. I couldn't wait to show my coaster its new home on my office desk. The pop of pink frosting with sprinkles would be a friendly addition to the dark wood. The happy colors brought very sweet memories.

Red and green are also happy colors in my book. I know each family has their own Christmas color scheme, but in our family, it's always been the traditional red and green. Clearly Starbucks agrees. At Christmas, the store is festive with seasonal décor and of course, the signature red cups, a little holiday for your hand as you venture out into the day. Though I'd opted out of decorating the first Christmas without Dustin, the season is always to be celebrated. As I stood in line one morning for my drink, I glanced at the various gift packages and Christmas-themed gift cards, but I was particularly drawn to the ceramic ornaments of miniature to-go cups adorning a three-foot tree. Each year it seemed there were new designs to choose from, and I'd always wanted one. Later that week as I was driving home from work, I let my mind wander to little red cups on a tree . . .

As with Christmas, our beverage choices differed as well. I loved coffee; he preferred diet soda. However, Starbucks had special significance for us because we logged a number of critical conversations at the location off I-35 in Temple. It was where early in our "friendship," we talked in the parking lot till 2 a.m. because neither of us really wanted to go home. I think we finally left because a cop car circled the parking lot twice assuming we were up to no good. It was where I first told him I loved him after making him wait days to hear it. Come to think of it, that also happened in the parking lot because I couldn't wait to get the words out once I saw him. I promise we did actually make it into the coffee shop on occasion, and over coffee and hot chocolate for him, he talked about asking for my dad's permission to date me (date not marry). To that I almost spit out my drink in shock, but in the end couldn't help but appreciate his chivalrous respect for family mixed with a healthy fear that he didn't want to screw this up.

Lastly, it was where I triumphantly sauntered with left hand slightly extended and tilted so the fluorescent lighting could dance off my diamond. After sharing the news of our engagement with family and friends, I declared that we must toast this occasion, but not with champagne . . . a tall, peppermint mocha, extra hot, light whip, at our place! *Since it was a celebration, I'm sure I opted for full whip.*

While I reminisced of coffee chats long gone, the car drove on autopilot toward a house void of festivity. At the point of my usual exit, I was overcome with misty-eyed momentum. My want for the little red cup ornament shifted into a need. I thought of how special it would be each year to hang the ornament as a reminder of many cups shared with Dustin. I had to have one, and I began to speed toward Temple. Nevermind that I passed two to three other Starbucks—likely fully stocked with the same ornament selection—my ornament had to come from *our* Starbucks. I felt like Santa on his sleigh racing toward my destination. It was a strangely happy moment with a sprinkling of Christmas magic. I proudly drove my red ornamental cup home while sipping an extra hot peppermint mocha out of the life-sized version. I promptly put the ornament in the closet with the other decorations and sat in my recliner savoring the conquest.

Every Christmas since, I look forward to hanging this souvenir of us in the perfect spot on the tree, a spot where I can see it clearly and remember fondly. I worry less about forgetting cherished memories because I have these small mementos to serve as time capsules for a brief, but blessed, chapter of my life.

16

In February of 2012, I found myself briefly in Palm Springs of all places. I flew into Ontario International Airport and drove through an hour-and-a-half of desert to find this much-famed oasis of golfers, celebrities, and palms that reminded me of my home in South Texas. But I didn't want to be there. To be sure, it was a childish and ungrateful response since I was there on the dime of my employer to attend a conference where we would be receiving an award. It was a privilege, really—not a conference we normally attended, but in light of the award, I would be allowed to enjoy the week of industry sessions and evening fun. However, when you're exhausted as I was and feel lost in your own home, you are exceptionally unsettled in a foreign place. The grief exhaustion had come back, and it was only with great effort that I willed myself to drag luggage and legs through the massive lobby of fragrant floral displays and shiny chandeliers to the temporary safety of my room.

I remember when I was notified about the award. Though we'd received recognition for the program before, this honor was particularly significant because it was from a national association. Looking back, I can't recall if I was initially contacted by phone or letter, but I distinctly remember the complete absence of enthusiasm or joy. This program was my work baby, one Dustin had helped me birth. Only weeks before his death, we'd received word of our first award for its success from a state association. I rushed home to share the news, and as we sat on the bed, Dustin took my hand and, in an uncharacteristically serious moment for us, looked intently into my eyes and told me how proud he was of me. The moment was only broken up by Izze walking ever so deliberately over our hands, swishing her tail back and forth in disapproval at the length of our embrace. She was Daddy's girl, and I was not to forget that. It was a short, simple exchange but a nice one, and the memory of it soured the moment at present. *This* award would be the one to rush home about and bask in his praise; but he was not there to tell, and the reality stripped the award of all worth to me.

It's a lesson in perspective indeed. How circumstances flip the lens of how we view life. When shared with someone special, the most mundane of tasks can become glorious while the limelight alone can be empty. From my balcony, I could dive into any one of the three beautiful pools framed by lush golf courses, but it all felt strange to me. I trudged from session to session and event to event in an uneasy stupor. Finally, on my last evening, I realized I wasn't going to naturally rise to the occasion, but in the words of my mom spoken regularly during my childhood, I would have to "choose my attitude." Life and for the moment Palm Springs was passing me by.

Lord, I need to go for a drive. I asked the concierge for directions to El Paseo, the Rodeo Drive of Palm Springs, and with each forced step of faith out the hotel, I felt anticipation grow. When I turned onto El Paseo, I felt I was driving down the street of a Hollywood movie. The sidewalks were lined with flowers, cafes, and windows showcasing an assortment of designer goodies. I drove until I found a parking spot that required no parallel parking between luxury vehicles worth twice my annual salary. *Exhale*. I made it.

Walk with me, Lord? Allowing yourself to enjoy and experience life again, even in small doses, can almost feel like taking those first few steps without crutches—expectant but oh-so-cautious. It helps when you know there's someone walking alongside you with a strong arm to grip should you falter. With a bit of flair, I swung the door shut and escaped into the moment on the arm of my Savior, a gentleman and friend, and as if to reward my brief return to myself, a sweet memory met my gaze. Although I recognized most of the stores I passed, across the street a sign, "Cold Nose Warm Heart," froze me in my tracks. *What could this be? Did they know?* And without thought to traffic or the logical explanation for the store's name, I abandoned my path and floated towards the mysterious store. In retrospect, there was nothing mysterious or magical about the store or its name, but it was a piece of Dustin sent to me on the streets of Palm Springs.

I wouldn't necessarily describe myself as cold natured, that is, except for my nose. When the temperatures start to drop, my nose retains the chill more than any other part of my body. Even after being bundled up in my infamous pink fuzzy robe with heat running, my nose is still ice to the touch. The frustrating thing about this affliction is that there's really nothing you can do about it. I have an assortment of winter accessories, but though we have gloves for the hands, scarves for the neck, and hats for the head, we have nothing that can be worn constantly over the nose—at least not without looking like you intend to rob a bank. Instead I've been known to clasp my hands over my mouth and nose and breathe hot air into the space for as long as I can get away with it without a stare.

I'm not sure when we made the discovery that Dustin was the answer to my nose's chilly predicament, but it was likely when we were cuddling one evening on the couch in my apartment. Below your jaw, on either side of your esophagus, there's the perfect soft spot, just the right size for an average size nose, and mine fit perfectly into Dustin's. On cold nights . . . and days . . . I'd bury my nose into his neck and be completely content. I think at first he found it amusing that I'd made such a discovery and that my nose was always strangely cold.

After a while, he accepted it as the new norm. Depending on the day, he might be greeted with a nose nestled in his neck before a kiss on the lips. For our wedding, one of our friends gave us a Willow Tree figurine of a couple encircled in each other's arms. It was a beautiful depiction of love, but what I appreciated most about it was that the tilt of the woman's head made it look like her head was snuggled next to the man's neck. Clearly, this woman had found a warm place for her cold nose, buried in the neck of her love.

Cold Nose Warm Heart. Yes, that's exactly how it would be described, and somehow this store owner knew. I would buy a souvenir here! Although it likely comes as no surprise, I was momentarily puzzled when upon entering the store I realized this was not a sentimental gift shop but a shop for very proud pet owners and their cold (wet) nosed, furry friends. *Of course.* I would find no heart-shaped keychains here, but I had my pick of any canine breed my heart desired framed in mugs, magnets, and aprons.

In my stubbornness, I still perused the store for a keepsake of the memory, but eventually surrendered with a chuckle to the irony of the situation, knowing Dustin would find this particularly amusing. "Serves her right for digging her icy-cold nose into my neck all those years."

No, I didn't waltz into a magical store of our memories in the literal sense, but on a Palm Springs street, miles from home, I was welcomed by something lovelier than the flowers that adorned the sidewalks and the jewels draped over carpeted displays in the windows. In the haze of travel and exhaustion, when I wasn't looking, the Lord gave me what I so needed—to feel close to Dustin in a place completely foreign to the both of us. My new life was becoming more and more distant to anything we'd known as a couple. It was new territory, places we'd never been, and sometimes it scared me. But a little pet shop in the palms reminded me that I could still take him with me.

17

I remember when I began my housesitting gig at our friends' home; I'd often retreat to the patio for a simple dinner, enjoying the cool of the evening with a book or laptop for company. Who am I kidding? I live in Texas, and in the summertime, there is no "cool of the evening." There is only slightly less sweltering and not-so-ovenous, but despite the weather, sometimes you just have to get away, escape your confines, and breathe. I'd been in their home only two weeks, and it was already a mess. How I'd managed to take what was not packed in the storage of our little apartment life and sprawl it across a four bedroom house was beyond me. More space definitely meant more mess, and the clutter just reminded me of all the things I had yet to do—organize, mail/write overdue thank you notes, and iron two baskets of laundry, just to name a few. But there was no clutter outside, no piles demanding my attention, no thank you notes worthy of sentiments I had not the energy to muster, just the rustle of the trees and the promise of an endless sky. I could think about everything or nothing at all, and that was a treasure even the Texas heat couldn't diminish.

However, life could not be lived on the patio. Work I could wrap my head around, but life beyond that remained complicated. Upon facing the proposition of an entire weekend all by myself, the first in that house, I made a few furtive attempts to conjure up plans with friends. Mind you, I didn't come out and ask. I just hinted and hinted, until even I couldn't stand the sound of my own desperation. It quickly became very apparent that I was meant to spend this weekend alone, as if God was saying, "Ok, now we try to start living." *Start?! What had I been doing the last four months?!* Surviving. The answer came to me. I was "surviving instead of thriving," though I didn't feel as if thriving was really on my radar.

A few weeks prior, a dear friend of mine, who knows me better than I know myself sometimes, had given me a unique gift for my birthday. It was quite comical actually to see her fidget nervously at our lunch date not sure when to present the item. Finally mid-conversation, she just threw the gift bag at me and begged me to open it and put her out of her misery. Having been a witness to the many unexpected triggers of grief, she was worried that she was about to present me with a live wire! I pulled the tissue paper out cautiously, glancing periodically at my nervous friend for cues. Inside was a custom-printed apron with a picture of Dustin and me on the night we got engaged. After breathing a sigh of relief that I hadn't broken down into tears, she explained that she really felt it was a God thing. Cooking had always been something I greatly enjoyed and something I should still enjoy, though I loathed the idea of it at the time. That afternoon, she was God and Dustin's self-proclaimed ambassador, delivering a gentle message, the hardest one of all—it's okay to start living. And to make the difficult process a little easier, she made sure Dustin would be with me in the kitchen.

It's true—cooking is one of my favorite hobbies. Planning for a meal or party gives me the greatest rush. I will pour over magazines and cookbooks searching out new recipes to try while taking maybe a little too much delight in making various to-do lists, organizing them by errand type: food, décor, or miscellaneous. I actually *enjoy* going to the grocery store, but then Dustin did too and more frequently than I, for that matter. Such is the life of the spontaneous, versus the planner. He most certainly preferred inspiration on the spot over my lists and recipes. Though we didn't always shop together, it took me quite a while to not walk the aisles of the store without the urge to pick up the phone and ask him how much milk we had in the fridge or add his favorites to the cart per our usual regimen.

In the early days, the autopilot kicks in every once in a while, and you have to stop and remind yourself that you no longer need V-8 or mineral water because there's no one to drink them at home. Those are the little things that get you and make the process of "living" very challenging. They are the private hurdles too small for anyone else to notice but big enough to cause a painful pause.

I stood a guest in the lovely kitchen loaned to me as a reprieve. How funny that a year earlier, my friend and I had cooked many a meal while our husbands laughed in the other room. That evening, like many before it during my stay, the stove remained cold. I stared at the thoughtful apron, back at the stove, sighed, and reached for the TV remote. This baby step was going to require some reinforcements, so I turned on the Cooking Channel to bring in the big guns. Watching cooking shows alone was a strangely emotional feat. In our evenings, we logged endless hours of Food Network programming, which prompted many experiments in the kitchen and dreams of a restaurant or food truck of our own.

I cautiously embraced my solitary confinement and dove head first into cookbooks, pans of simmering sauces, and an impromptu baking session that resulted in two dozen softball sugar cookies for my niece's team. Nearing midnight, I finally surrendered, exhausted with hands cramping from a new decorating technique and flour turning my once-black leggings gray. I collapsed into the bed not caring that a splotch of icing still stuck to my arm and savoring the recollection of time with someone I once knew . . . me. And so began a summer of getting reacquainted with a beloved pastime. Together with Rachel Ray, Giada Di Laurentiis and a host of other familiar faces, I whisked, whipped, and sautéed my way back into the kitchen.

18

One man's trash is another man's treasure . . . and if I may, his wife's clutter to clean. Dustin was always one to spot hidden gems. Initially, it was one of the reasons I fell in love with him—his Christ-like eye for the lost. However, shortly into our marriage, I learned that this salvage spirit applied to things (junk) as much as people. His ideal Saturday morning often involved trips to the flea market and to my dread, purchases of questionable value and origin. I tried to be a good wife and dutifully listen as he took random items from a plastic sack and explained how he'd brokered a deal for the "valuable" item. It was how we ended up with a food dehydrator, a Strawberry Shortcake clock, *three* antique meat grinders, and a clarinet, among countless other garage sale orphans.

I know they teach you in marriage, as in life, to pick your battles. Needless to say, I'd surrendered long ago to the fact that one day when we had a garage of our own, it would likely be overflowing with Dustin's projects, all of which only needed "a good cleaning" to be ready for the Craigslist stage. I remember the day he walked into our apartment announcing proudly that he'd purchased the clarinet. A clarinet.

On this day, I did not back down. *We're buying clarinets now for two people who couldn't play an instrument if their lives depended on it?!* When confronted with the ridiculousness of his purchase, he adamantly shook his head and said he only paid $12 for it. *Great, twelve dollars on someone's junky clarinet that will take residence in our closet within weeks.* Unfazed, he gently placed the case on our kitchen table. With a twinkle in his eye, he lifted the lid—dangling handle and all—as if he was unveiling the crowned jewels. Though all five pieces were present and accounted for in their place, I was still less than impressed.

But, oh, he'd been waiting for this moment. He'd anticipated my skepticism and bubble-bursting looks, but this time he knew he'd hit the jackpot. With great satisfaction, he told me about his trip to the music store on his way home from the market. His curiosity was rewarded when the clerk not only acknowledged the excellent condition of the instrument but informed Dustin that he could probably get $250-$300 if he were to sell it. There it was. We were finally going to make money on one of his discoveries, not Antiques Roadshow kind of money, but hey—any profit, and particularly profit in the hundreds, was worth celebrating! This would be a first for us, so celebrate we did, and I made sure to give my American Picker ample credit for his keen eye. He'd later go back to the music store and purchase reeds and mouthpiece cleaner for the new owner. *Goodness knows how many mouths had touched that thing on its way to the Hwy. 190 Flea Market! Eeew.*

Of course the clarinet never made it to Craigslist as intended. Our long-awaited shot at a successful profit was permanently delayed by the tragically unexpected. I hauled that broken case with me on several moves, and it rode around in my trunk forgotten until finally resting on the top shelf of my closet. Because it did have potential value, I tried to sell the instrument once or twice. Both attempts were unsuccessful. I'm the one person who never took their obligatory year of band in middle school and was not aware that purchasing instruments is seasonal. Again the shop owners confirmed its value, but I would need to come back before the start of the next school year.

It had been two-and-a-half years, and one day while driving by a school parking lot full of children eager for the new academic year, I realized I'd once again missed my window. I thumped the steering wheel in frustration. School was starting and by that point most students had already purchased their instruments in preparation for the start of school. Still, I figured I had better at least try to see if the band stores were biting, or the clarinet was doomed to collect dust for another year, maybe five, before I finally got around to posting it on Craigslist. I was hedging my bet on the slackers and procrastinators.

Later that week, I was scrolling through Facebook for a quick update before bed when a post from my sister-in-law caught my eye. "Does anyone have a clarinet they'd like to sell me?" I gasped and quickly re-read the post. *I have a clarinet! I mean I think it's a clarinet. Is it a clarinet? Heavens I don't know.* I hopped out of bed and ran to the storage closet, rummaging through the piles for the black box with dangling handle. I opened it and stared once again at the pieces. Thankfully, Dustin had the forethought to buy reeds because the packaging stated very clearly: clarinet. *Aha! I do have a clarinet!!* I ran/floated back to my room and immediately dialed April. I could barely contain my excitement.

April: "Hello?"

Me: "I have a clarinet!!!"

April: "What?" (To be fair, my words were gargled with giggles of joy.)

Me: **"I have a clarinet!"**

April: "Why do *you* have a clarinet?"

At that point, I was able to share with April the beautiful backstory of how this clarinet found its way to our home at her brother's hand. I could tell she was moved and overwhelmed at the thought. It appeared my ten-year-old niece, Reagan, had decided to play the clarinet that year, but in all the hustle and bustle of the summer, no clarinet had been purchased, to my frugal brother-in-law's dismay. Last minute purchases can have pricey consequences.

I paused, soaking it all in, and said, "Dustin bought Reagan a clarinet!" We both just paused and took in the beauty of the moment. He would've so loved knowing it ended up in Reagan's hands. He had a special place in his heart for little Reagan, and this . . . this was perfect, almost poetic. All these years, the clarinet sat in the closet waiting to be played, waiting for Reagan. That night after sisters rejoiced, I sat and reveled in the moment. It was one of those pure moments of joy you don't rush, and I'd certainly missed those in recent years. April texted me to say that I'd made the family's night. Reagan, a sentimental soul, loved the story, and said, "Mom, we can *never* sell it."

No, it can never be sold, not now, and I know it never will be.

19

I'm sitting in the living room staring at a vase of tulips on my coffee table. They have fully bloomed at this point and are actually on their way out, but I'm waiting till the last minute. I've come to love tulips, and I'm not quite sure when that changed because they used to be one of my least favorite flowers. I couldn't stand the way they snaked in all different directions as though trying to escape the vase. It bothered me. I wanted stationary flowers that stood at attention, kept in order, and maintained poise. To me, their sporadic nature made them unruly and less beautiful

I had tulips at my wedding. Maybe that's when the love affair began. They are synonymous with spring and therefore fit well into the March outdoor wedding scheme. My bouquet was stunning—light pink and white tulips adorned with fragrant sweet peas. It was the essence of romance. As to the tulips for the table centerpieces, they were to be packed into a square vase, standing upright like a picture I'd seen in a magazine.

However, when we arrived at the wedding venue that day, there were only a few tulips per vase, and they reclined in the vase, forming a swoop. In retrospect, it was still very pretty, just a different artistic spin, but it combined with the bright pink bows around the smaller vases sunk my vision of what the reception tables were supposed to look like. It was not Bridezilla who followed, but rather a distracted bride who wanted nothing more than to be enraptured with the magic of the day but found herself struggling to shake the irk.

At one point, I sneaked out to the back patio alone to make the frantic phone call. It must have ranked as one of the more ridiculous cries for help I'd made to him because truly what man really cares about the positioning of tulips in a vase on his wedding day? And how on earth is he expected to have a solution to the problem? Of course, I wasn't expecting him to fix the problem of the disappointing centerpieces; I was expecting him to fix his crazy bride! I needed him to make it better like he always did when I'd fly off the handle about something equally life-altering. He was a safe place for me where I could let the craziness in my head loose while he lovingly talked me off the ledge or made me laugh at the absurdities of the concocted scenarios in my head. Poor guy, you'd think he deserved a break on his wedding day, but in true Dustin fashion, he gently helped me see what really mattered (though I'm sure I heard the hint of "*Really?!*" in his voice).

I still think back on that moment and the precious moments wasted fretting over flowers, "needing" them to be just so, and losing my focus when they weren't. To do it all over again. If hindsight in general is 20/20, then hindsight after death is 20/60. The clarity is compounded by the unbearable sting of regret and the fragility of time. I'd never thought of myself as a perfectionist. I just liked things a certain way. But at what cost? Had life turned out differently, I might not even remember my squabble over the centerpieces, or it would be a funny story at dinner parties. But I didn't realize we'd have so few moments ,which makes each moment wasted devastating. I'm still very much a believer in doing things with excellence, but maybe it's not the end of the world if your house is not spotless when someone stops by unexpectedly needing to talk . . . and you let them in instead of pretending you're not home. Maybe. It's at least a start.

On what would've been our two-year anniversary, I received two dozen tulips from a friend. Though it was a multicolored bouquet, the bright and blush pink stems bound together made me cry as I remembered my wedding bouquet. I received other flowers that week, some of my usual favorites from before, yet I was surprised at how I was drawn to the tulips, which had already begun to stretch in various directions. I loved their unique structure in that there was none. They naturally veered towards the light but even then made their own way. As pretty as the roses were, I found them too perfect.

Why do we do that—focus on the minor flaws, the specs, and the out-of-place? We see the one tiny thread dangling from the shirt, and pick and pull till our fingers are tangled in masses, and behind is left a noticeable tear or snag from a tiny thread that would otherwise have gone unnoticed. We just can't help ourselves. Or can we?

I've come to learn it's a two-part process, these transformations. For one thing, I have to choose to pursue the change that might otherwise be laughed off as a familiar "personality flaw." It's a common scene at girls' nights or brunches—the conversations surrounding the endless list of foibles and weaknesses we can't seem to shake. "Oh, I have absolutely no patience . . ." "I'm such a perfectionist . . ." "I just wish I wasn't such a people pleaser . . ." Though our words indicate a desire for change, our actions reveal we've actually embraced these labels as a part of who we are and let them dictate our day-to-day lives. So I've realized the first step is to take these troubling traits seriously and serve them notice.

The other half of this process is where the change really happens. It's the constant prompting and tugging going on behind the scenes. It's the gradual revelations God brings through life's circumstances, people, or nature. The way He gently but firmly tells us to take note of His direction because He's offering us an opportunity to change. These revelations can be subtle hints, or in the case of the tulips, heartbreaking realizations when the trade-off is considered. Truly this journey since losing Dustin has been like navigating quicksand; and if not careful, God's revelations can be skewed into chains of guilt and regret instead of the gift of freedom they were intended to be in our lives.

As I admire my lovely bouquet, I celebrate the change. The change that happens gradually and then, in moments like these, is realized. If given the opportunity to go back, I'd jump at the chance to respond differently and spare myself the forever sting of that moment. But now I realize that I'm blooming too, and I'm learning to trust the process. A few years ago, I felt lifeless, but there's been much pruning since. The hard dirt has softened, giving life to new growth. I too reach for the light, and His healing rays ensure that beauty blooms from the ashes.

20

He said he'd found "a bike as old as his wife's soul," and indeed he had. Propped against the back wall of the back room of a downtown trophy and engraving store, Dustin spotted a gem hiding beneath years of rust, chipped paint, and dust. How we even found ourselves in the back room of this older gentleman's store, I don't know, but there we were, surveying the tools of his trade, personal collectibles, and stacks of bills next to a half-eaten sandwich from lunch. We'd only stopped in because the "Going Out of Business" sign in the window was a beacon to my husband's hidden treasure-finding heart. I followed him into the store dubious of any sort of payload waiting for us amidst the last remaining medals and sports trophies, yet within minutes, Dustin had made a new friend.

As they talked, I knew Dustin was canvasing the room for bargains, but I smiled inside at the tenderness with which he spoke to the man about his life's work, allowing him a moment of pride in this final chapter of a lifelong occupation. It was Dustin's sincerity that always drew people to him. He genuinely wanted to hear their stories, no matter how small, scandalous, or seemingly insignificant, and people trusted him with them. I felt for the old man and hoped somehow this business closure would be the start of something new and exciting. He seemed tired, and the empty shelves made me sad while the items in my husband's hands gave me cause for concern. In one hand he held two belt buckles, and in the other, a large conch shell. The belt buckles were unique—I'll give him that—but I wasn't quite sure where the giant conch was going to take residence.

"Do you have anything in the back?" he said.

Dustin! I couldn't believe he'd just invited us into this man's private work area that I'm sure doubled as his private quarters on some days. The man ran his fingers through his floppy gray hair, shrugged his shoulders as if to say "why not?" and led us through the door marked PRIVATE. *Good grief.*

The back room was large and dimly lit, but Dustin's hunch did not disappoint. There were a number of antique items lying around that began to peak my curiosity. Of course I longed to hear the story behind them—who used them and what was life like when the items were considered new. I'm a sucker for a story, and I'm fairly certain antique salesmen see people like me coming a mile away. They know if the story is believable enough and peppered with delicious details of another time, I'll eat anything they cook up . . . and pay for it too! I didn't see the bicycle at first because I was enamored with the retro refrigerator, circa 1950, off to the corner in the makeshift kitchen. Now that was a glorious appliance! What it likely suffered in utility, it well made up for in vintage glory. Dustin saw it too, but it was not for sale nor did these newlyweds have a place for such an item in the apartment complex that already had a fridge. Nevertheless, an offer was made and promptly rejected.

"How about that old bicycle? Is it for sale?" said Dustin.

The other side of my sucker-for-a-story self is my aversion to haggling. If by chance I manage to eek out some modicum of bravery and request a lower price, I will cave the instant my offer is rejected. I'm liable to pay extra in an effort to backpedal my apparent impudence and flee all confrontation. I certainly don't ask to buy things that aren't for sale! Dustin saw things differently.

I thought for sure we'd worn out our welcome with the bid on the fridge, but then I followed his gaze to "that old bicycle" and fell in love. I immediately swallowed my rebuke and watched Dustin work with wide-eyes and a shut mouth. The old man didn't respond at first, but after a few minutes of silent hesitation, he wheeled out the bike into the cloudy rays of the fluorescent light. Its lines were sleek, and the leather seat was firm. The tired blue paint, cracked wheels, and rusty handle bars testified to years of use, perhaps years of love. I wondered if we were bidding on something too precious to let go of, despite its obvious neglect. My suspicions were confirmed when he began reminiscing of riding the bike in its heyday . . . WHEN HE WAS ELEVEN. Goodness gracious, there was no way we could take this bike; it was a piece of his childhood! Yet I wanted so desperately for it to be mine. It was a true classic, and it had a story.

Weeks earlier when Dustin brought home expensive mountain bikes donated by another member of the church, I was only mildly enthused. I had long romanticized about owning a vintage bike someday, complete with wicker basket, a bouquet of flowers and a warm baguette. I would not only picture the bike but myself riding through the picturesque countryside or a quaint town en-route to the farmer's market with my straw hat shielding me from the sun. (Helmets don't quite lend to fashionable daydreaming.) Yes, if I was going to take up bike riding again in my late twenties, it would have to be wrapped in nostalgia. The little ninety-year-old woman inside me wouldn't have it any other way.

Back in the shop, the man was still deliberating. Dustin pulled me aside and told me to go across the street and purchase something, anything, but make sure to get cash back. Cash in hand was king for impromptu negotiations. I didn't want to leave the action, but he insisted, so I dutifully made my way to an actual antique store across the way. The bells above the door chimed of a different time and alerted a kind, middle-aged woman behind the counter. I smiled politely and forced myself to make an obligatory walk around the store, stopping occasionally to admire an item and appreciate its history. Normally, I would've enjoyed the stroll through the centuries, but I was preoccupied with thoughts of the negotiations taking place across the street. I can't recall what item I settled on, but as soon as I emerged from the store with a package and cash, my husband and his new friend were stepping into the sunlight with bike in tow. Dustin was beaming. "Take it for a spin!" he said and then whispered, "And give me that cash! Two people have already stopped to ask about the bike, wanting to counter-offer."

At that point, I couldn't tell if he was basking in my joy or the affirmations of strangers, jealous of the amazing deal he'd brokered. I suppose it was both, and the combination had him floating off the ground. I mounted the bike with Dustin's help and pushed hard against the heavy pedals. There were no changing gears on this baby, but I quickly found my rhythm. As I rode down the sloped street, it was not 2011, it was 1950. I was wearing pedal-pushers and a glow you could see for miles. My beau had just won the ultimate prize for me, and all the other poodle skirts could just watch with envy from the sidewalk! Yes, this was what dreams were made of; this was young love, care-free and timeless.

It was like bringing home a new baby. On the drive back to the apartment, we both took turns calling parents and friends. My calls were of a more romantic nature, while his to my father-in-law were more braggadocios, detailing the sale, offer by counter-offer. The apple hadn't fallen far from the tree. When we arrived home, we introduced the kitties to the newest member of the family and hoped they wouldn't be too jealous that the bike was already given its own room on day one.

Dustin bought me the bike of my dreams, and it was by far the best gift he'd ever given me. He talked all that evening of how he was going to take it apart and restore it so that it was truly a vessel worthy of his wife. I told him I wanted it painted red, just as I'd pictured it in many a daydream. Red, he said, it would be! The restoration had commenced, and with it went my living room. For weeks on end it seemed the floor of our already confined space was covered with rims, spokes, handle bars, and pieces of a once-blue frame. He meticulously cleaned, sanded, and repaired, but when tired, left all the pieces where they fell. It really couldn't be helped I suppose. We had no garage, and this one-of-a-kind bike could not be trusted to the elements on the back porch.

However, with each passing week the clutter tested the magic that was already under stress from changes in both of our jobs and the first year learning curve of marriage. In some ways the state of the bike mirrored our then present state of mind. It seemed like we were fiddling with the pieces of our new life trying to see how they all fit together, and occasionally in our exhaustion, we just let them lie where they fell. Sometimes that's just what functioning looks like. You step over the pieces or scoot them to the side because you just don't have the energy or presence of mind to pick them up. Bike parts were all over the place, and at times, it felt like we were all over the place too. Just as I'd about reached my breaking point, he walked into the apartment one afternoon with a bicycle horn to melt my heart. I can't remember if he special ordered it or found it at the swap meet, but it was perfect. I could hold out for the restoration a little bit longer.

But what I thought would be a seasonal project ready by spring languished for months and ultimately fell to me to complete. The restoration of the bike, such a loving gesture, would later become a labor of love by friends and strangers instead . . . love for me and love for Dustin. I was left to raise this child on my own.

I moved all the freshly sanded parts to a corner of the guest room while I sorted through the pieces of life post-March '11. They no longer excited me. Salt on a very fresh wound was all they'd become. But as weeks turned into months, I found myself vacillating from resenting the bike one day to obsessing over its completion the next. It was such a beautiful memory, and I knew he'd want to see me ride it one day, if God allowed such things. At the time, I liked to believe He did.

The summer days were growing longer, and since I would be moving soon, I became desperate not to lose the parts in the shuffle. The next step in the restoration process was paint, and I knew Dustin had already approached a man in our church who owned a car body shop about having the bike professionally painted. He was determined for it to look as good as new while allowing the patina on the handlebars to allude to its age. It was certainly not something I could do on my own. I would be forced to ask for help, something I loathed. In grief, I discovered my people-pleasing nature to be a chain binding me to some false ideal that I could do it myself. I hated the thought of so many being inconvenienced because of me. Once I'd surmised in the brief weeks following Dustin's death that everyone else's lives go back to normal, I was hesitant to disrupt their norm to help me navigate the baby steps of my new existence. I was often frustrated by my helpless state.

But helpless I was, particularly when it came to assembling an antique bike. It was something I had neither the skill nor heart to complete. I had to surrender the pieces, messy as they were, in hopes that one day, when rebuilt, the bike would be wholly restored and ready to ride again.

So the next Sunday, I approached Alan after church with the resolve to ask him about painting my bike. I knew this was an unusual request, so my nerves got the better of me. I quickly began to ramble, recounting needless details about the bike's discovery and Dustin's intentions. I observed that this was awkward for him as well, not in the sense that he was uncomfortable with my grief, but more so that he knew the weight of the request being made of him. I was entrusting this precious piece of Dustin to him, and he smiled kindly as I continued in my ramblings to make sure he knew I intended to pay, and on and on. I think he felt led to put me out of my misery so he interrupted me with an emphatic "Yes, yes, of course, Amanda!" It had been some time, but he did remember Dustin calling him. He would be happy to do it, and I was to come to the shop that week to pick out my paint—my red paint.

When I arrived at the shop, I had butterflies in my stomach. Alan bounded out of his office with smiles and followed me to the car. I opened the trunk as though lifting the lid of a treasure chest.

"Let's see what we've got!" he said as he peered into the trunk. "Hmmm. Yep! We'll get this all taken care of for you Ms. Amanda. Now come with me and pick out your paint."

Within a week, I received the call that the paint was set, and the parts were ready for pickup. I jumped out of bed like it was Christmas morning to get to the shop when it opened. As Alan led me past the office to one of the car bays, I felt the other employees watch me with a glint in their eyes. I assumed they knew the story behind the random bike parts, and I felt their anticipation for the reveal. I didn't disappoint. I'm sure they heard my squeals of delight through the closed door. I've always been a gift squealer and not one to contain my enthusiasm. A friend once told me she wished I could be her translator when opening gifts so that I could portray what she felt inside but didn't know how to express. Wouldn't that be a funny exchange? *What she really means by her casual smile and demure "Thank you so much" is "Woohoo!! This is exactly what I've needed! How did you know?!"* (Cue hands in the air and spontaneous hugs for the gift giver.) That morning in the shop, no coaxing was needed; my heart was filled with joy at the sight. The red was perfect, and the lacquer gave each piece a brilliant shine. As I reached for my wallet, Alan waved away my card. There would be no charge. I stood stunned, overwhelmed by gratitude. Though I thought I'd taken this burden upon myself, the Lord was showing me His sweet provision, as if to say, "Let me do this for you, daughter." Alan was promptly introduced to the spontaneous hug.

It was time to assemble, the final and by far most important step in the long process. I'd researched a couple options, but as you can imagine, most bicycle shops keep to the big cities. Be that as it may, a new small business specializing in bike repair had opened off the expressway on my way to work. I decided it was time and loaded up the freshly painted frame, wheels, and random accessory pieces, laying each one gently on a towel in the trunk. It was like transporting ancient bones.

The shop had high ceilings and the rear wall slid back like a garage door so road warriors could ride on up inside for a quick fix or chat. I sat patiently by the register allowing the other customers to be served before me so I could rehearse my request over again in my mind. Plus, the fewer people in the store the better. I wanted to minimize distractions when it came my time to speak. I watched the owner as he tended to the others in a happy-go-lucky manner, much as you'd expect from the owner of a bicycle shop. He was likeable to be sure, but I was more interested in his knowledge than pleasant demeanor. Unfortunately, my bike didn't come with instructions, and all I had was a picture we'd taken that first day to show that somehow all these pieces went together.

"And how can I help you, ma'am?" he said as he wiped tire dirt from his hands and fiddled with the casually arranged displays.

I turned my stool to face him and leaned in, face stern. He didn't realize it, but he was being interviewed for a very special task. I was going to lay it on thick. He would know I was a widow of only a few months after only a year of marriage. I needed him to listen intently. I would tell him of Dustin's grand romantic gesture and lofty intentions, cut tragically short. He needed to know the bike's story. I'd allow my guard to fall so he could see exhaustion, lingering shock, and sadness. I needed him to know this meant everything to me.

I had no intention of getting emotional, though tears tempted the corners of my eyes as I built my case to compel this stranger to take my bike. The money wasn't an issue. I'd have paid a thousand dollars gladly if that was the tab. No, I needed to shake that man's hand and walk away knowing his hands could get the job done right and honor the memory entrusted to them. As I spoke, I felt a little sorry for the man. Though he remained calm and listened respectfully, I could tell he was unsettled by the sad story coming from a woman half his age. I sometimes forgot that though I'd told the story a hundred times, for most, it was their first time hearing the account.

He looked at the picture for a good while, and I told him we believed it was a Western Flyer, a bicycle manufactured between 1930 and 1950. I waited and audibly exhaled my relief when he agreed to take the job. I could tell he wasn't one for sentiment, but he did his best to assure me that he'd take great care with it and not rush the process. I was fine with that. We carried the bones gingerly out of the car, and he directed me to take them to a room adjoining the shop. The area was to be rented by a masseuse, but for now, it would be a safe place to keep the parts separate so they wouldn't get mixed up with another order. This man of few words blessed me greatly with his actions as he gently laid each piece on the bed instead of the floor and made known to the other guys that this room was not to be disturbed. I drove away with a strange mix of emotions like that of a mom dropping her child off at camp, not exactly sure what I'd find upon my return in a month.

When pick-up day arrived, I was once again forced to ask for help. The bike was not likely to fit in my VW Jetta, and I felt a bit obsessive about its safety on its first trip to our temporary home. I recruited my co-worker, Laurie, who we affectionately called "Mom" for many reasons, not least of which was her soccer mom van that often carted the group to lunch. While the van made her an obvious pick, she was also exactly the person I needed that day. Her other mom duties that year included many a counseling session over long walks in the park. I say counseling, but more often than not it was just listening. She listened, and as she listened, I could tell she was trying to learn. She didn't come to our conversations with fixes or advice; she came with two ears and a very tender heart. I treasured our walks, and in many of those early months, lived for them. It was like being able to exhale after holding my breath for eight hours at the office. Yes, Laurie had a van, but it was her heart that made her the ideal chauffer.

I chatted aimlessly about randomness at work as we drove, trying not to think too much, and slough off the weight I felt for what I was about to do. It wasn't how the unveiling was supposed to be, but then nothing really was anymore. I knew that but tried to be grateful that I would have this piece of Dustin to treasure when I needed a tangible reminder of our time. I walked into the shop tentatively and looked around. There it was. After almost a year of being disassembled, it was complete. Our Western Flyer had been loved back to life, and she was indeed a beauty! I recall being strangely quiet, almost solemn in my appreciation, like no one else was in the room. I think I later summoned some visual excitement for the benefit of the owner who'd stood back and watched, apprehensive of my reaction. He said a few customers had wanted to buy it. That didn't surprise me. It was perfect.

Once fastened in, Laurie and I drove in silence. Again she listened and waited for my cues. I kept my hand on the bike the whole drive, and once we arrived at the house, I was anxious for her to leave so I could ride. It was such a bittersweet moment, but it was time.

Though she now looked almost brand new, the stiff gears affirmed her age. I made a mental note to have them adjusted when I returned for the wicker basket. It still required some muscle to move the pedals forward, but each labored push fueled my spirit. Despite the initial effort to get going, I soon found my rhythm and felt like I was flying. I charged into the wind and let it whisk my hair behind my face. I reached for the horn and squeezed the bulb multiple times not caring who heard. I needed that sound to reach heaven.

Someone had been waiting a long time to hear it.

ACKNOWLEDGEMENTS:

I am a rich woman. You might not guess that if you drove past my quaint three bedroom home or took a spin in my functional Volkswagon Golf, nor does my bank account lend to that assertion. However, in my lifetime I have amassed great wealth in friendships—the kind that are good as gold, refined by the fires of life and lasting throughout many years. To my girlfriends—you know who you are—you have made my life rich, my laughs deep, my joys full, and my hurts bearable. This book is a celebration of your love and companionship because, in many ways, you helped carry me to this point. You who dropped everything to fly hundreds of miles to be by my side. You who wrote me notes, sent me texts, and sat with me for hours. You who prayed for me and with me day after day. You who loved me when I was weird and wondered what the future held. Not all of your stories are included in these pages, but your love is reflected in its completion.

Thank you to those who had a direct role in the journey

that was *Learning to Ride Again.* Courtney Strong for your strong blend of accountability and encouragement, cheering me to the finish line. Mom, for a childhood of impromptu grammar lessons; the reminders paid off! You supported me in writing this book as you have in every other stage of my life, giving me the honest feedback and unconditional love only a mom can give. To my Aunt Stephanie Dickinson who I entrusted chapter after chapter to her author's eye and soared from her uplifting words.

To the women of Fedd Books who believed in me, heard my voice in the pages, and guided me through the maze of publishing to share this story with the world. This season with you has been a joy. Lauren Hall, thank you for helping my words shine and hearing my heart. After all, someone has been waiting to hear it . . .

To Dustin's family who granted me the permission to write freely and loved me deeply through the process. You trusted me with your son and brother in life, and I hope I have honored him in death.

BIO

Amanda Stephens grew up in South Texas and though a world traveler, keeps Texas her home. As a young girl, she wrote to pen imaginary stories and dreams. As a woman, she writes to tell her own and offer hope from a place of personal healing. She currently resides in Salado.

ENDNOTES

1. William P. Young, *The Shack* (Newbury Park, CA: Windblown Media, 2007) 24-25.

2. *The Bucket List*. Dir. Rob Reiner. Screenplay by Justin Zackham. Perf. Morgan Freeman and Jack Nicholson. Warner Bros., 2007. DVD.